Suzie Woodward's
WARDROBE STRATEGY

SUZIE WOODWARD'S
WARDROBE STRATEGY

Printed in the United States of America.

10   9   8   7   6   5   4   3   2   1

ISBN 0-89426-051-0

The Scientific Press
540 University Avenue
Palo Alto, CA 94301
(415) 322-5221

For Bert Woodward, my late husband . . .

whose contribution to this book and my career extends far beyond
what one would expect of a mentor, a friend, and a husband.
He gave of himself completely, that I might become my best me.

ACKNOWLEDGMENTS

I have adored doing this book, but it would never have been born if Paul Kelly had not provided me with the opportunity, the place, the time, the people, the love, and the encouragement.

I am happy to have shared the experience with Elaine Fritz whose tireless efforts and excitement for the subject matter made writing a joy; to Laura Hamilton for taking care of the office so beautifully while I was deeply into the project; to Peggy Rose for the encouraging anecdotes and Saturday proofreadings; to Gene Smith for setting type with such talent and precision; to Joan Muller who has been by my side for over eight years sharing in all of the hard work, pressure and fun of *Wardrobe Strategy;* and, above all, to my son Tom, who believes in me and who ungrudgingly provided me the freedom of time in which to write and who spurred me on by believing in me with so much love.

Contents

Preface

I became curious about how people dressed when I was a little girl. I used to sit in a chair in my mother's sitting room and watch her get dressed to go out with Daddy. He always thought she was beautiful no matter what she wore, but I noticed that he acted a little friendlier when she wore certain things, and was sort of polite and formal when she wore other things.

For twelve years I had to wear a school uniform. I'm convinced that this requirement was the source of my fascination with wardrobe. In our uniforms we all looked the same and everything depended on our individual personalities, but once a month we had Civilian Day when we wore "real" clothes. Our reactions to one another changed drastically on that day. A girl who was usually a class leader might wear a print dress, and I would go home wondering why she seemed so much more fun than usual. I noticed that, for no apparent reason, I was sometimes a bit more intimidating in my regular clothes than in my powder blue uniform. I began to realize the power of clothes, and became addicted to the psychological analysis of wardrobe.

As I grew up I began to see clothes as a valuable tool that few people understand—they simply buy the clothes that they are attracted to without realizing how they affect the people around them; they never realize that the reaction they get is not always the reaction they want.

I began to catalog the looks that I saw people wearing, noting the responses they created in people. I narrowed it down to seven basic looks, and I realized that each of these looks create separate reactions that everyone might like to have some of the time.

My fascination with clothes also led me to explore fashion history, and I discovered that clothing styles occur in predictable cycles. This is a controversial idea, because fashion designers have no sense of following a cyclical schedule in their creativity, but time and the passing of these cycles right on schedule has shown the usefulness of this theory.

This book was written to help you accurately predict the line of the clothes you should buy for the next several years, choose looks that meet the psychological needs of particular situations, and use color in your clothes effectively. It will also teach you how to analyze your figure shape and use the best lines for your body type, and how to shop for a satisfying wardrobe that will prove to be a solid investment of your clothing budget. Here's what each chapter covers:

Chapter 1   Gives you a little drama that illustrates all the ways *not* to buy clothes, then points out the Four Shopping Sins that most of us have indulged in to our eventual regret.

Chapter 2   Gives you a way to analyze your body type and tips on choosing style variations that will be visually flattering.

Chapter 3 Gives you everything you need to know about the Three Cycles, so that you can avoid buying clothes that are about to go out of style and invest in a wardrobe that will last for five years.

Chapter 4 This outline of the Seven Looks classifies all the ways you can put your clothes together to achieve your interpersonal goals. I explain how men, women, and children react to each look and how to vary the looks with accents from other looks.

Chapter 5 You don't need to be a slave to your "color palette"—and this chapter teaches you how to wear colors that are not in your color group. You will also learn what effect the color of the clothes you wear has on other people, and how men and women differ in their reactions to color.

Chapter 6 Gives you a lifestyle formula to follow in planning your wardrobe for each career, social, or home setting you need to dress for.

Chapter 7 Tells you how, when, and where to shop, and outlines the Sophisticate Method— a surprising approach to shopping that will give you a versatile and exciting wardrobe that you can build on over the years.

There are several ways you might use this book. You could become your own wardrobe expert, mastering each part of the theory and making a detailed plan for acquiring a wardrobe that meets all your life-style needs.

You might also use it to help you understand the psychology of clothes—to check whether the way you dress is meeting your interpersonal needs. Most women's wardrobes are primarily concentrated on a single look, one that is either high or low in power, with the result that they do not present themselves well when they need other reactions.

If you'd like to have a wardrobe specialist help you do your shopping, the training you get here will help you use your expert's time effectively. There are many wardrobe consultants around the country, and I would be glad to recommend one near you.

I also publish a bimonthly newsletter, filled with tips on shopping for the current cycle and articles that expand on the theories in this book. If you would like to subscribe, use the coupon at the back of the book, or contact me:

Images by Suzie
540 University Avenue, Suite 325
Palo Alto, CA 94301
(415) 326-4646

May all your future shopping trips be happy and productive! Good luck!

Suzie Woodward
Palo Alto, California
September, 1984

1. The Four Shopping Sins

Today is Monday! In just one week you're going to leave for a long-awaited spring holiday in Europe with your husband. You have mixed emotions about leaving your two children for a whole month, but you're delighted to have time to share new adventures with your husband, and you'll finally be able to introduce him to your favorite business associates abroad.

Because of your busy schedule—French lessons at the university, your job at the bank, Little League games, ballet recitals, business dinners, organizing meals and day care, and out-of-town business conferences, you've had too little time to prepare yourself for this trip. With one week to go, today is the day you have set aside to plan the last-minute details of your wardrobe.

Even though you went shopping a month ago for a convention in Los Angeles, you discover that many of the items you purchased will not be right for this trip—you want to look your best in Europe! In fact, for some reason you *never* have the right clothes. Of course, every once in a while you hit on an outfit that works well for your lifestyle, but usually you're frustrated because you seem to spend a lot of time and money without finding a look that suits you.

And, speaking of money, your charge accounts seem always to be up to the limit, but you have little to show for what you've spent. Your husband and friends are puzzled by your constant complaints about having nothing to wear even though the bills continue to cover your desk in the family room. This subject has been a bone of contention between you and your husband for several years, but luckily your persistence has outlasted his irritability. After all, you're a successful woman and you want to feel attractive so you can be relaxed and free from "appearance worry." And you also know that when you're not pleased with the way you look, it's hard not to be moody and irritable.

Have you noticed that men don't seem to have the same wardrobe problems that women have, either in business or social life? You never see men panic when a trip is on the horizon. They always seem to have the right thing to wear and they spend very little time putting their wardrobe together. In fact, the average man spends only a quarter of the time a woman does in coordinating clothes. Today, you envy your husband's simpler wardrobe.

Well, this time will be different: You're going to go shopping, and without spending a fortune, you're going to buy just a few things that will make you look spectacular on this vacation.

You've scheduled a whole day. The kids will be taken care of by a neighborhood teenager, you're caught up at the office, and you've taken special care to prepare dinner in advance so that things will be well organized if you're late returning from your shopping spree. And you've invited your well-dressed friend and business associate Elizabeth along, because her opinion has helped you many times in the past. Perhaps some of her good luck will rub off on you.

Because you've been so organized, you feel a great sense of pride as you drive to Elizabeth's house. Today you will finally find a wardrobe you will enjoy in Europe and in your business life when you come home.

It's 9:30 a.m. as you arrive at Elizabeth's. The stores aren't quite open yet, so you and Elizabeth decide to stop for a quick cup of coffee to discuss your plan of attack. Elizabeth hasn't eaten yet, so she orders a complete breakfast ("and then we won't have to stop for lunch"). This takes another twenty minutes, and then you have to wait for the check. Oh well, it's only 10:30 a.m.—no problem! "We still have all day!" says Elizabeth.

You choose the first store because you remember a certain outfit you bought there a few months back. You liked it pretty well, so you go back to the same department to try to repeat the feeling of that style. But this time you see many unfamiliar styles, and as you finger the clothes on the racks, you say to Elizabeth, "Where would I ever wear that?" or "Tom doesn't like me in yellow." Suddenly you and Elizabeth feel as if the store's merchandise is somewhere between chaotic and confused. You wonder if you've just gotten too used to shopping in your neighborhood shopping center.

You cheer yourself up—it's still early! Perhaps they've moved the *good* stuff to another department. You go up to the next floor. Again you feel as if the clothes don't make sense, but you do find two or

3

three things you want to try on. You're aware that Elizabeth is patiently pacing up and down outside. As you try on three different outfits in the dressing room, you wish you'd lost the eight pounds you gained in Los Angeles. A suit skirt fits, but its jacket is too small. A dress fits, but the fabric is too clingy. A blouse is great—but you can't think of anything to wear with it. In the meantime, Elizabeth finds another dress you might like, and then crows, "Look what I found to try on! I've been needing a new spring outfit for a long time." Your mood gradually changes from excitement to *PANIC!* After all, you *have* to buy something!

The dress Elizabeth brought in wasn't too bad. Perhaps if your hair were brushed out and loose, if you had on the right lipstick, and if your shoes were bone instead of navy—maybe the dress would work out all right for a couple of evenings. It's a little more than you wanted to spend, but ". . . just this once," you murmur to yourself.

Now for the shoes. You need something you can walk comfortably in, so you decide to check the shoes on the second floor—they've always been nice to you and they have good, quality brands. On your way to the escalator you see a group of women crowding around a sales rack and are diverted. Each of you finds two or three different blouses with great markdowns. You try them on and—bingo!—they work. You buy them. (You can always use the beige blouse for the office, and your white blouse is just about worn out, and you can't beat the price!) Now for the shoes. . . .

The dialogue: "I'm sorry but we just sold the last pair of bone shoes in that style. However, I would be *happy* to place an order for you—it would only take three weeks and we can just charge them and send them to your home when they arrive."

"No thanks, I need them for a trip this week."

You ask to see what else they have in that color tone, and the salesman brings out several pairs. You finally settle on one. You tell Elizabeth, "They're not quite what I wanted, but they're comfortable and they'll be nice for walking!"

Pleased with your success, you both feel a bit hungry in spite of your vow to skip lunch, and you decide that a glass of wine will help you relax while you reassess what you've accomplished and what you still need to complete your wardrobe.

While you lunch, Elizabeth announces her decision to get a divorce and wants your advice on how to handle some of the problems she'll have. Lost in conversation, you both lose track of time; the next thing you know, it's 3:00 p.m. But you're not ready for your trip yet!

Once again you and Elizabeth trek through the stores. You find a nice pair of pants (although you already have fifteen pairs) and some pretty pearl earrings. Before you realize it, it's 5:30 and time to drive home, drop off Elizabeth, have dinner with your family, and show your husband what you bought for the trip.

The very next day you go to your closet to figure out what to pack, and suddenly you realize that you *still* don't have the clothes you pictured yourself wearing so confidently in Europe. In complete frustration you exclaim that you *hate* to shop because you never find anything you like to wear. Your husband shrugs —he knows that you spent almost $300 yesterday and that he has lost more space in the closet. He's wishing he didn't have to complicate your life with vacations and other outings that give you so many problems with your clothes.

If this scenario sounds familiar, let me assure you that your experience is shared with most of the women I meet in my seminars and classes.

Chances are you are reading this book because you want to get the best possible wardrobe in return for the money and time you put into building it. There's a term for it: *investment shopping*. Buying clothes is an investment just as stocks and bonds are—if you buy wisely, your wardrobe will be worth a lot. If you do not do long-term planning and consider your personal investment needs, your portfolio of clothes will not be worth as much to you.

Investment shopping is the term we will use to define the approach of someone who wants the advantages that come from planning a flattering wardrobe that will last for a long time.

Forget all your previous ideas about shopping. I'm going to show you how to be an investment shopper—and I'll begin by telling you about the *Four Shopping Sins*. These are the commonest shopping errors people make in building their wardrobes.

Let's backtrack and discover what our shopper could have done to have a more successful shopping day and a better planned wardrobe.

Sin #1:
Occasion Shopping

The shopper just described is a classic example of the Occasion Shopper. What is it that makes us want to look better on a vacation than we do at home? After all, most of the people we meet on vacation will never cross our paths again, while the people we live around are an integral part of more permanent alliances. *Their* opinions about us matter, because our reputations are at stake in our local business and social circles.

I remember a time in my life when I had to buy a new outfit every time I went on a trip with my husband. It didn't matter if we were going to be gone two, four, or ten days—it was something I did automatically. Now you and I both know that when you're wearing a brand-new outfit, it takes a bit of time to make it feel like *you*. More often than not, you find that the outfit you left at home would have been more comfortable, and in fact would have looked *better* on you than the one you rushed out to buy two days before you left.

Even worse, when you return home, you may find that this particular purchase doesn't fit your lifestyle and hangs hopelessly in your closet—a constant reminder of a mistake that it's too late to rectify.

From childhood we are used to planning our wardrobes based on occasions: We buy a graduation outfit or a going-away-for-the-summer wardrobe; we go on a shopping spree to get ready for college; and of course we buy a trousseau when we begin a new life as a married woman. This basic approach stays with us throughout our lives and is capitalized on by retail businesses. Often the decision to buy something new is more for our psychological benefit than for our physical needs.

Retail stores exploit the psychology of Occasion Dressing to stimulate people to shop several times a year. The more you're in a store, the greater the chance you'll buy something. The shopping year is divided into Holiday Wear, Cruise Wear, Mother's Day, and so on—all designed to encourage you to be an Occasion Shopper.

Most Occasion Shoppers have a great deal more in common than their overcrowded closets. In my experience with many women in all different walks of life, I have found that the most common problem they have is that of having the right garment for a given occasion without spending a lot of time and money. They have a feeling of boredom when they discuss what they have at home in their closets, and imagine that other women have much more exciting clothes to wear. It is this attitude that sends them to the stores for a day of shopping, often just for something to do.

It is when shopping becomes emotional that a woman leaves herself vulnerable to confusion, frustration, and eventually boredom. Moods change quickly, and stores and designers are there to encourage you to become a fashion victim—someone who buys indiscriminately every time an occasion arises.

This panic buying can be avoided when you have a wardrobe organized well in advance to fit each and every new and unusual situation. Granted, there will still be times when you want to shop for something special, but this is an exception to your basic wardrobe plan; if you only wear it once or twice and discard it, you haven't hurt the workability of your long-term program.

Sin #2:
Single-Item Purchasing

Another common mistake many women make is to go shopping for a specific item, with a limited amount of time and money to spend. Retail merchants encourage single-item purchasing in order to increase the number of times you're in the store—you have to keep coming back to finish putting together a particular outfit piece by piece.

If the original item you purchase—for example, a dress—has a simple line change that deviates from the style of the rest of your wardrobe, you will be unable to make the new garment work interchangeably, so you'll have to make a lot of additional purchases to complete the new look.

Sin #3:
Sale Shopping

Is this one of your secret sins? Our Occasion Shopper allowed herself to be sidetracked by a sale. A rule of thumb I often use with my clients is that if you wouldn't purchase it at full retail price, don't buy it just because it's on sale.

If it isn't worth the full price, then why should it take up space in your closet? Unless your eye is highly trained, you can be tricked into purchasing something that will go out of style soon after you've paid the bill.

Sales are often a sign of poor buying on the part of the department store buyers—why should you have to pay for their mistakes by making them your own, at whatever astonishing markdown? If women stopped buying sale merchandise, prices of decent goods would get lower and you would be able to find the items you want to have in your wardrobe much more easily.

Sin #4:
The Psychological Sin of Insecurity

One of the biggest mistakes women make is to compare themselves to other women that they imagine are more fashionable. An insecure woman may yield to the temptation of buying exactly what another woman has in her wardrobe in order to avoid feeling unattractive next to her more confident associate. The result is usually to become an imperfect copy of the other person—her physical and personal characteristics are different, and when the insecure woman looks in the mirror and sees the unsatisfying result, her self-doubts are confirmed.

Women who suffer from insecurity are particularly susceptible to the pressure of peers who do not like to have the "average" way of dressing challenged. This is a form of group insecurity, but groups often set and maintain unspoken boundaries to keep anyone from being too outstanding.

Have you ever overheard a group of women talking about an absent friend who has a reputation for being very well dressed? The entire group works hard to find something she doesn't do right. This is the only way they can bring her down to their level so that they feel less intimidated by her confidence and creative individuality.

When we see someone that seems to do everything with great taste and creativity, most of us want to emulate her particular look, but fall short. For her it is an innate talent, and she is comfortable in expressing that part of her personality through her dress. We may not feel as confident because we have not learned to define our personal style and taste preferences.

To define these terms, *taste* is individual preference, while *style* is the fashion characteristic of a particular period. Almost everyone dresses in the current style, but not everyone has developed her way of making that style individual. Any woman can buy the latest dress, but not every woman can make that dress look original. Most of us are too lazy to take the time to complete our look using our personal tastes.

The culture we live in imposes its will on all of us in many subtle ways—through movies, television, books, advertising, school, personal contact with one another, and the conventions and ideals of the past that our parents pass on to us. Our culture inherits and sustains some very inhuman and unrealistic pressures, including its attitude toward fashion and the way we dress.

Despite these pressures, an emotionally healthy and secure woman—like you!—can create the freedom to feel and to express her individuality while remaining within the cultural norm.

Because of these four Shopping Sins, your closet may be junked full of clothes that keep your wardrobe from fitting your daily needs. Your lifestyle demands versatility and good looks at a minimum cost to your wallet, and clothes that produce a minimum of "getting-ready stress."

A Sampler of Insecure Attitudes

There are many attitudes that can prevent you from enhancing your visual presentation. Underline the ones that apply to you.

1. I might make a mistake.	You *will* make a few mistakes while learning to enhance your visual presentation, but taking the time to learn how to organize your wardrobe now will save hours of unnecessary stress later.
2. Someone might not like the changes.	You can be quite sure there will be someone who won't like what you've done. People get used to an interpretation and are often envious of your success. This can be a matter of taste—and not everyone can wear the same things.

3. Someone might criticize my appearance.
If they haven't criticized your appearance in the past, they probably won't critize you now. Criticism, if delivered by a knowledgeable party, can teach you useful things.

4. I might make someone else uncomfortable.
Every time you are with another person who lacks confidence, you are a reminder to them that they would be better off if they sharpened their wardrobe skills.

5. I can't afford to reorganize my wardrobe.
You've probably always been able to afford those things you've *really* wanted in the past. Perhaps your wardrobe budget needs reassessment. Knowing what and how to make your wardrobe workable will always save you money.

6. It isn't important enough to me.
You haven't yet experienced the rewards of self-esteem. Once you have, it will be very important to you.

7. I'm perfect already.
By whose standards? There is always room for knowledgeable improvement. The more attractive you become, the more you will understand the value of learning.

8. I don't have the time.
If you take the time now to learn how to build your wardrobe, the well-organized results will save you many hours in the future.

And Now—
Investment Shopping

In working with women all over the country, I have come to realize that part of the confusion about dressing occurs because women's lifestyles have altered so much over the last twenty years. When we were all homemakers, getting dressed had very different requirements. Our lives were simpler and didn't require the versatility that moving constantly among the world's of business and home and motherhood demands. We may not have had a lot of money for clothes, but we didn't have to be serious about budgeting a versatile wardrobe.

As for any investment you make, you must do a great deal of research to insure that your clothing investment will be sound over a period of time. You must consider your lifestyle and future plans, and review what will be happening in the fashion industry for the next several years.

I discovered something very interesting in my research of fashion and wardrobe trends for men and women: *Fashion trends and lines are cyclical.* In digging back through modern fashion history to see whether this discovery held true, I found that in many areas of the United States, wardrobe trends evolve in periods of about five years. Most people are not aware of this because they shop only for their short-term needs—the *occasion,* observing only the season in which they are making their purchases.

When I say to my audiences, "What does the word *classic* mean?" they respond by saying, "Something that lasts forever—like the blazer." But I have found that there is no such thing as a classic, even among blazers. Because of style trends, blazers have changes in lapels, pocket placement, fabric, and number of buttons. Which blazer is the classic—the one with one, two, or three buttons? The one with notched lapels wide at the shoulders, or the one with the low, narrow lapels? Each cycle has slightly different details.

During the beginning of each five-year period or cycle, we find a dramatic change in fashion trends. How does the fashion industry encourage women to buy a whole new look? One of the best ways to sell a new idea is by bringing it into the stores in the finest quality at a reasonable price. This merchandise is what I refer to as *first-piece goods*. If, in the first year of a new fashion trend, you buy first-piece goods, you have a wardrobe investment that will wear well for five years.

While most women are complaining about the changes and waiting for them to go out of style, I am in the stores buying up quality first-piece goods to build my wardrobe on for the coming five-year period. When the complainers finally realize that the trend is going to last, two years have passed and they have to pay a premium for merchandise of less quality. At that point, I will be winding down my buying while they are just getting started; my wardrobe will be worn out at the end of the five-year period, while their clothes will still be in good shape but going out of style. In wardrobes that I visit professionally, I find a great deal of waste because of this resistance to fashion change.

I believe that the bulk of the money invested in your wardrobe should be spent during the first two years of a trend. The last three years should have low budgets, and evidence of new trends will already be visible to the trained eye. Most women don't budget their wardrobes at all, and when they purchase only a piece at a time, they end up spending twice as much money as they should for their clothes, while limiting the versatility of their wardrobes.

Investment shopping, therefore, is best described as the process of working within the framework of the three five-year cycles (described in Chapter 3), based on a specific budget that will be spent during the early part of each five-year cycle, and decided by the needs and goals of your lifestyle during that period.

For the woman who doesn't have the time or desire to study investment dressing, there are image consultants all over the country who can do the research for you and help you put your look together. You go to professionals to balance your accounts, clean your home, teach your children, take care of your car, and handle your legal problems. It's also smart to go to a professional wardrobe consultant to organize an appropriate look for your demanding business and social life.

2. Your Body Type

If you want to take responsibility for your own image, the first step to take in planning a well-organized wardrobe for yourself is to evaluate your physical characteristics—as well as your attitudes about your physical appearance.

In my lectures all around the country, one of the most universal phrases I hear is, "I can't . . . ." We all seem to know quite well what it is that we *can't* do, and nearly all of our limitations are based on our analysis of what our figure flaws seem to be.

But figure analysis is a tricky thing. Most of us can't see ourselves objectively and we often believe we have detected flaws that other people don't even notice. Taking measurements is helpful, but it really only gives us proportion differences, and many people have trouble relating that to how clothing fits anyway.

It *is* important to define your figure's characteristics, however, and one of the most helpful ways to do this is to get a friend to outline your body on two large pieces of butcher paper. Lie down on the paper, wearing a leotard or swimming suit, and have your

Figure analysis is a tricky thing; most of us can't see ourselves objectively.

friend draw a line around you two ways: on the first piece of paper, lie down on your back with your hands at your sides; on the second piece, lie on your side with your underneath hand extended above your head. Then fill in these two outlines with black paint or a felt-tip pen, and you will be able to see your figure proportions clearly.

You may have arrived at your beliefs about your figure by comparing your measurements with those of your friends, but this can be misleading. The only useful figure interpretation you need for knowing how to dress is the actual proportion your figure has to itself. One helpful way to think about the lines you should wear is to decide whether you have an A-shaped, T-shaped, or H-shaped figure.

Defining and Balancing Your Figure Shape

If your shoulders are narrower than your hips, you have an *A-shaped figure*. If, on the other hand, your shoulder line extends beyond your hip line, you have a *T-shaped figure*. An *H-shaped figure* has hips and shoulders that seem to be the same width, but you H-figures usually have a very small waist. If you have done the life-sized outlines of your figure, you can simply measure and compare the distance across your shoulders and hips and decide which of these three body types you have. Now let's talk about what this means when you choose your clothes.

The A-Shaped Figure

If your figure is an A-shape, with shoulders narrower than your hips, you probably also have a large bustline. This creates special problems because of your narrow, often sloping, shoulders. The *single most important secret* for A-shaped figures is to add a shoulder pad to your blouses and jackets. This leaves enough ease for the bustline and prevents blouses from popping open at the bust. It also helps balance the hipline and gives most women with this figure shape a much better fit in all their clothing. Typically, A-shaped women wear a smaller size on the top than on the bottom, which can make buying a wardrobe very difficult.

The single most important secret for A-shaped figures is to add a shoulder pad to your blouses and jackets.

Another problem I have found with A-shaped figures is that they are often short-waisted. These women need to wear wide belts, because narrow belts simply disappear in the folds of their figures. Another belt trick they should use is to match their belt color to that of their blouse, because it will then visually lower their waistline. For example, if you wear a white blouse and red skirt, a white belt will make your top half extend to the bottom of the belt; if you wear a red belt, your waist starts at the top of the skirt's band, and not only do you look even more short-waisted than ever, but the belt disappears and has no accessory value.

To get the most from your figure proportions, you A-shaped women should wear your blouses and skirts in the same color. You can accent this monochromatic look with any color belt you want because people will see you as a taller, slimmer, better proportioned woman than if you divide your look between two colors.

The T-Shaped Figure

With your shoulders already wider than your hips, you do not need to add large shoulder pads. Most T-shaped women do not have large bustlines, but if you *do* have a full bust, shoulder pads will not help you. You need to provide balance by wearing full skirts, and you can accentuate your small waistline by using interesting belts, either narrow or wide.

T-shaped women ... you need to provide balance by wearing full skirts.

The T-shaped woman usually has a problem with either a pouchy stomach area or a very rounded bottom. From the side, she has almost a b-shaped or d-shaped figure. If this describes you, you should look for clothes that are slightly gathered above the problem area. If your stomach protrudes slightly, then you will do well in skirts that have gathering in the front. If you are a d-shape, which means that your bottom protrudes slightly, then you need skirts that have a slight bit of gathering in the back. The dirndl or A-line skirt are the two best lines for you, and whenever you wear a straight skirt, it needs to have some gathering in order to fit your proportions comfortably.

When you buy blazers or jackets that you intend to wear buttoned, I would suggest that they be at least a two-button jacket. The length of your jacket should extend to your wrist area when you hold your arm straight down beside your body. Avoid short jackets—they will only accentuate your problems.

Your best pant style will not have a fly-front zipper, but when this can't be avoided because it is a major fashion look, be careful to choose pants with darts and a set-in zipper.

The H-Shaped Figure

If you are an H-shaped woman with shoulders and hips about the same width and a small waist, you have a choice of wearing shoulder pads or not, depending on how much exaggeration you want in your wardrobe's look. You should use a variety of belts to accent your small waist, especially if you are that rare H-shaped woman with a large bustline. In this case you may want to use shoulder pads, but you have to be careful not to over-exaggerate your look to the point of appearing top-heavy.

H-shaped woman . . . you should use a variety of belts and accent your small waist.

Women with an H-shaped figure often have short legs and a long upper body. This becomes a difficulty when narrow-legged pants are in fashion, because they draw attention to short legs. If this is true of you, you can extend the length of your legs by wearing a basic pant shape with a long, tunic-length jacket or blazer.

Another technique that works quite well is to wear opaque stockings that match or contrast with your skirt and shoes. If you wear a white blouse with a navy skirt, you can choose navy stockings and navy shoes to visually extend your legs' length. It also works to wear opaque white stockings with a navy skirt, white blouse, and navy shoes, because the eye combines the white blouse and stockings, and the navy skirt and shoes, and sees a long line—a very balanced and flattering way of combining your wardrobe items. What you *can't* do is wear a navy skirt, navy stockings, a white blouse, and shoes of another color, because that visually cuts the length of your legs at the top of your shoes.

Almost all figures have problems; you can limit your wardrobe and feel frustrated, or you can learn to present your figure in a number of different looks.

It may comfort you to know that almost *all* figures have problems. You can choose to limit your wardrobe lines and feel frustrated, or you can learn to work with accessories and complementary lines to present your figure at its best in a number of different looks. Here's a surprising fact that I've taught my clients over the last ten years: *For your figure to look its best, you often have to accentuate your flaws.* This goes against all we have been told for years, but I've found that it almost always works.

An example of this is what you just read about dressing an A-shaped woman who has narrow shoulders and is short-waisted: I would accent her shoulders with shoulder pads, and add a wide belt even though she's short-waisted. With the addition of these two accents, she will appear much better proportioned and her clothes will seem to fit her more comfortably.

About Height and Weight

Most women have the misconception that being short or tall limits their wardrobe choices. This is absolutely not true!—height is simply a matter of relativity. If I am 5'5" tall and you are 5'3" tall, you will appear to be short in relation to my height. However, both of us will look short if we're standing next to someone who is 5'8" tall. All my research and work with clients continues to lead to the same conclusion—height is only relative to the person you are standing beside.

The only really important thing is proportion. If I have three women standing side-by-side, all of different heights and all having A-shaped figures, they can all wear the same clothing lines, cut, of course, to fit their height.

Furthermore, if an A-shaped woman wears a size 14 and then loses weight and becomes a size 6, she can still only wear things that are proportioned for an A-shaped figure. She does not become an H-shape or a T-shape just because she has lost weight. Of course, she may look better in her clothing, and she may *feel* so much better that she wants to wear more wardrobe variations, but her basic figure shape will remain exactly the same—it will just be smaller. Diets simply can't alter bone shape, but they *can* make you feel better about yourself.

If you eat like a bird and still gain weight, you are probably an *A-shaped* figure. Overweight in this body shape can never be blamed on heavy bones. Your bones are small and neatly padded, so they don't stand out in relief. Neither do your muscles. All your body contours are rounded and smooth. A-shaped figures tend to have round, wide, large faces supported by relatively short necks. Your waistline is high and your hips and bust are full-sized. No matter

Most women have the misconception that being short or tall limits their wardrobe choices. This is absolutely not true.

how much weight you gain or lose, your bust, waist, and hips will have the largest dimensions in proportion to the rest of your body.

The *T-shaped* woman is the envy of all other figure shapes because you are the ones who have the most difficulty gaining weight. Your motor muscles and digestive tract are small. Your body fires burn more intensely than those of other body builds and a large proportion of your food is used up through nervous drive. It is best for you to increase the number of meals you eat to as many as six per day so that your body can retain the energy you need to get through your day's activities. When you *do* gain weight, it will tend to settle in your stomach area, but this isn't usually noticeable until you reach middle age.

Squareness and solidity mark the *H-shaped* figure. If yours is a rectangular, squarish body, hard and solid, in a sturdy frame, you have the classic H-shaped body. This body shape eats to live and can digest more food per unit of body weight than other builds because your big muscles spend energy galore. You can go for a long time between meals, but when hunger strikes, it is fierce. You have a tendency to wolf meals down and therefore can gain weight if you decrease your exercise. When you put on weight, you have a tendency to gain evenly in your shoulders and thighs, and to become even more square; it is easy for your body to take on a masculine build. The H-shaped figure is the only body build that may be able to slim by exercise alone. When you were young you were probably very physically active, but danger lies ahead for the H-shape who, as she grows older, tries to keep up the same eating pace without keeping up her exercise regimen.

And while I'm on the subject of diet: One of the things I've learned from working with clients is that losing weight just before buying a new wardrobe can be a very expensive venture. Most women I know maintain their weight at a certain level without trying. That level is usually where they have the most energy and don't have to continually struggle to control their weight.

Losing weight just before buying a new wardrobe can be a very expensive venture.

Admittedly it's much more fun to buy clothes after you have shed some of the weight you've wanted to get rid of for years, but what happens to all those expensive clothes in your closet when you give up the constant struggle and return to your former weight? Clothes can always be made smaller, but it is difficult to make them bigger. I usually suggest to women that they shop when their weight is up, because we can always alter clothes when their weight loss becomes noticeable and stable.

Disguising Your Figure Problems

If you're like my clients, you probably have most of your fashion hang-ups in the area of figure analysis. I can assure you that the fashion industry provides a wide variety of camouflage for those little figure eccentricities of yours—why not try a few on for size?

The fashion industry provides a wide variety of camouflage for those little figure eccentricities of yours . . .

27

If You're Short-Waisted

Use shoulder pads in your blouses and jackets to make your upper body appear longer.

Epaulets or any kind of shoulder detail are attractive on you.

Don't wear dolman sleeves or dropped shoulders unless you add shoulder pads.

Jacket styles that work well on your figure are Eisenhower jackets, shorter blazers that end at your hipbone, and belted overblouses. Make sure your blazer button hits at the waistband of your pants or skirt, never below the level of your waistband.

Wear blouses that are the same color as your skirt or slacks to carry the eye beyond your waist. Vests in the same color as your skirts or pants look nice on you for the same reason.

Avoid large pocket detail above the waist.

Wear wide belts. Wear obi-style belts, wide in front and narrow in back. Try a double-wrapped belt that goes around your waist twice. Choose a leather belt of the same color as your blouse, with the buckle in either silver or gold.

Buy belts in heavy materials such as leather, because most fabric belts will not hold their shape on you.

If You're Long-Waisted

Belted overblouses look very nice on you, especially if you have the blouse in one color, the pants or skirt in another, and your belt matching the bottom half.

Very short jackets are difficult for you to wear; however, some of the variations that are good for you are the long Eisenhower jacket or vest and the Chanel jacket or bolero look.

Make sure that your sleeve lengths are correct for you. When you bend your arm at a 90-degree angle, your blouse cuff should end at the wristbone and your jacket or coat sleeve should leave an inch of blouse showing.

You can wear your necklaces and scarves long—over the bustline or even longer. Exaggeration of this line is very flattering on you.

You can wear either wide or narrow belts, and asymmetrical looks in belts and waistbands are attractive on you. Match your belt color to your skirt or pants.

If You're Thick-Waisted

Use shoulder pads to help disguise your waist. Make sure that the waistbands on your skirts and pants are slightly wider than usual; this gives the appearance of a waist, even if yours is hard to find.

Dolman-sleeved or dropped-shoulder blouses make your waist look wider, but you *can* wear dolman-sleeved sweaters when they have tightly knitted, wide waistbands.

Don't buy dresses that have gathered waistbands, and don't wear self-belts that are narrow and poorly made.

The look of coat dresses and chemises is nice on you unless you have a large bustline. Don't wear Chanel jackets; they widen your waistline.

Choose belts that have heavy textures such as leather, Ultrasuede, and nubby fabrics, and make sure they have interesting buckles in silver, gold, or a color. If you're long-waisted, match the leather part to the color of your skirt; if you're short-waisted, match it to the color of your blouse.

If You Have Full Hips

If you also have narrow shoulders, wear shoulder pads in your blouses and jackets to balance your hipline.

Skirts that have a slight gathering in the back are flattering on you.

Skirts or slacks that are bias cut at the side will hang beautifully on you. To tell whether a garment is bias cut, just pull the fabric at the side of the skirt or pants: If it has give when you pull the fabric up and down, it is bias cut; if it resists the pull, it is not cut on the bias.

With slacks, you should wear tunic-length jackets or blazers. The most appropriate tunic length for you comes to the bottom of your middle finger when you hold your arm straight down and extend your fingers down. A shorter tunic length for you would end at wrist-level when your arm is in this position.

If You Have Short Legs

Don't wear shoes with ankle straps. This cuts the leg line visually and shortens it further. Whenever possible, wear shoes in the same color as your hemline.

When you wear colored or opaque stockings, exactly match your hemline color and shoe color. This visually extends the leg. Alternatively, match the stockings to your blouse color, and keep your skirt and shoes the same color.

Your legs will appear longer if you wear your blouse and skirt in the same color.

Avoid overly long tunics when you're wearing them over pants or a skirt in a different color.

If You're Small-Busted

Avoid shoulder pads in your blouses; they'll make your bustline even smaller. Too much gathering or tucking at the top of your blouses will also narrow your bustline. Pleating at the bust is quite attractive on you.

Make sure that the bust darts on your blazers and jackets hit directly at your bustline, not above or below.

Dolman or dropped-shoulder looks are very nice on you.

You look best with your blouses left open at the top. V-necklines are very flattering to a narrow bust.

Wear necklaces and scarves that hang at the bustline to draw attention to that area.

Large overblouses are not your best look unless you choose soft, clingy fabrics.

If You're Full-Busted

Wear shoulder pads in all your jackets, blouses, and sweaters. They will improve the fit of your clothes and visually balance your full bustline.

On all your blouses, make sure that one button is at the center of the bustline, not above or below; your blouses will be less likely to pop open or strain across the front.

Choose interesting collars to take the viewer's attention away from the bustline. Wear jewelry at the neck area; long, hanging necklaces will only accentuate the bust.

Whenever possible, wear an underwire or minimizer bra.

Wear blouses and skirts in the same color tones.

Choose six-button double-breasted blazers instead of the two- or four-button variations.

Avoid large patch pockets at the bustline. Bustline smocking will also not be good on you.

If You Have a Rounded Stomach

When you choose pants and skirts, make sure there is some gathering at the front. But don't wear elastic waistbands in skirts, pants, or dresses, because they accentuate this problem.

Make sure that all your jacket or blazer lengths come to the hipbone or below, and be sure they can all be buttoned comfortably.

Don't choose double-breasted jackets with two or four buttons; you must have the six-button double-breasted look, or a jacket that has the shape of a double-breasted blazer but is actually buttonless.

Avoid knitted or clingy fabrics.

Peplum jackets and blouses, belted overblouses, and overbloused sweaters are all very nice on you.

Drop-waisted dresses and jackets will be terrific in your wardrobe, and so will smocked or waistless dresses.

For your belts, choose soft fabrics like Ultrasuede and heavy-duty cloth rather than leather or metal.

If You Have a Rounded Bottom

Your pants and skirts should have a slight gathering in the back for best fit. Straight skirts are difficult for you to wear, but skirts with square pleats and vents are very attractive on you.

Wearing skirts and jackets in the same color help to camouflage your figure.

Your best jacket styles are the bolero, the Eisenhower jacket, the Chanel jacket, and the fitted vest. Make sure that your blazers and jackets don't hit the top of your derriere and pucker. Don't buy blazers with open vents in back, because they'll spread open and emphasize your problem.

The chemise will not be a good line on you unless you belt and blouse it. Blouson-type dresses and blouses are nice on you.

Epaulets on blouses and accessories at the neck help to attract attention away from your bottom.

Don't wear too high a heel—it will only accentuate your bottom area.

If You Are Sway-Backed

You do very well with the blouson look and Eisenhower jacket styles. Tunics and long sweaters are also good on you. A small shoulder pad can add ease to your dresses and blouses, and they're always necessary in your blazers and jackets.

Make sure your slacks have darts both in front and in back; this will create a better fit for you. Don't buy skirts or pants with elastic waistbands.

Make sure your hemlines hang evenly all the way around.

Avoid jumpsuits; but you can achieve the same look by wearing color-matched pants and blouses.

When you buy dresses, don't wear the self-belt sold with the dress if it's just a narrow fabric belt.

The belts you choose should have substance, and most of the interest should be at the front. Remove belt loops from your slacks and skirts so that you can add belts with more depth.

Textured fabrics above the waist work well for you. For example, a cotton knit sweater with a linen skirt or a mohair vest with a gabardine or wool skirt or slacks would be very good on you.

If You Have Large Thighs

A-line and dirndl skirts are the most flattering for you. Don't wear short jackets with straight skirts; choose slightly longer jackets for them.

Don't wear straight-cut tunics unless you accentuate your waist area. When you belt your tunics or over-blouses, make sure they're bloused slightly around the belt.

Remove side pockets in dresses or skirts, because the extra bulk accentuates the thigh area.

Use a variety of accessories to take attention off the leg area—necklaces, scarves, interesting belts and earrings.

If You Have Large Calves

Use textures and accessories above the waist in order to keep the viewer's attention on the upper part of your body.

Your hemline is very important. It should hit you at the leg indentation at the top of your calf. If you wear long skirts, I suggest that they should hit you about two inches above the ankle rather than at the calf itself. When they're in style, look for dresses with uneven hemlines; you can wear them.

Knickers are not a good look for you, but split skirts are okay if you wear them with opaque stockings.

Opaque stockings are terrific on you, especially if you choose colors that exactly match your skirt and shoes. Never wear white or off-white opaque stockings; they would only exaggerate the problem.

Don't wear ankle-strap shoes; they'll draw too much attention to the leg. Plain, open-toed pumps are very nice on you, especially if you have a pedicure and your nails are painted a nice color. Very flat shoes are less flattering than shoes with some kind of heel. Don't wear two-toned shoes; solid colors are much more flattering for you.

Finding the Right Styles for You

A very important thing to remember when you're choosing your clothes is that every single wardrobe line has several versions. With your figure characteristics, you might be able to wear as many as five variations—if you can find them. For example, there is at least one version of the double-breasted blazer that works for each of the three figure types.

Every single wardrobe line has several variations; you might be able to wear as many as five.

35

If you are an A-shape, you can wear the six-button, lined, double-breasted, tunic-length blazer with either a self-belt across the back or an open vent in back, and the blazer should have shoulder pads.

If you are a T-shape, your best double-breasted blazer is the two-button version, buttoned low at the hip-bone. It could be lined or unstructured, and the more texture the better. It will look best on you without shoulder pads.

If you are an H-shape, you should wear the four-button double-breasted blazer, lined, with an open vent in back, and with patch pockets. Shoulder pads are optional for you.

If you're like many of my clients, you've tried on a double-breasted blazer that was wrong for you and assumed that it's a look you can't wear. We can't all wear the *same* versions, but if you look carefully there is always one possibility that will work beautifully.

Keep in mind that small retail stores can't possibly carry all of the available variations of a line you want to add to your wardrobe; if you want to be successful at finding the version that will flatter *you,* shop in large department stores, preferably in a city rather than in a suburban shopping center; these stores usually have as many as twenty of the fifty or more possible line differences.

Are you the sort of woman that becomes frustrated or depressed when you try on a fashionable look that doesn't work or fit properly? It's time you tried a new tactic: Instead of giving up on that look, ask yourself *why* it doesn't fit and what you could do to make it work for you. This positive attitude alone will give

Instead of giving up on that look, ask yourself why it doesn't fit properly.

you a much better sense of what makes things hang properly on you, as well as stimulate your creativity when you put your wardrobe together.

Take the example of an A-shaped woman trying on a dress with an elasticized waistband, belt loops, and a belt in matching fabric. There is no way a dress like this will flatter an A-shaped woman. To make it work for her, she must cut off the belt loops and throw away the matching belt. Supposing the dress is in solid navy, she could add a navy Ultrasuede or leather belt with a gold, silver, or textured buckle, and her unflattering dress now looks like it fits well and is expensive. If the dress is in a print, she should choose a belt in the dominant color, again using an interesting but complementary belt buckle. The belt in either case should completely cover the elastic in the dress, both for a polished look and to prevent the dress from riding up and looking matronly.

You should creatively adapt your accessories, too. If you don't have a long neck, but have found a very long scarf in just the right colors, cut the scarf in half. (It really won't bleed!) Keep one half for yourself and give the other half to a friend that lives in another part of the country. Now you don't have too much fabric around your neck—and you've made a friend happy too!

How to See Yourself in Proportion

Where do you stand when you look at yourself in a dressing room mirror? You *should* be standing at least four to six feet away from the mirror, because that's about how other people see you. Most of us stand too close and analyze every freckle, every hair out of place, every flaw we imagine to be twice as bad as it actually appears to those around us.

In fact, people see you as a single image; their eye cannot at a glance detect every flaw or figure line that bothers you. It's the overall image of your finished look that they remember, not every minute detail of your physical presentation.

It's the overall image of your finished look that people remember, not every minute detail of your physical presentation.

We've discussed one kind of proportion—understanding your body's profile and creating an overall balance by choosing the right clothing lines for your particular figure. But you also need to develop a sense of balance in size, color, and texture in order to present a polished image. If the overall picture appears to be out of proportion—even though you've managed to cleverly disguise your large hips and narrow shoulders—the image you present will be uncomfortable to look at.

As I travel around the country giving wardrobe seminars, I spend a lot of time in airports; I use my time to informally study what all kinds of women are wearing. There are a lot of well-dressed women out there—but too many of them come within an inch of looking great, and just miss. It's usually because they don't fully understand proportion. If you master the subtleties of proportion in your own presentation, you'll always look wonderful regardless of your height and weight. I'm going to give you three examples of combinations that are out of balance. See if you can spot the flaws yourself.

If you master the subtleties of proportion, you'll always look wonderful regardless of your height and weight.

1. She's wearing puffy sleeves, a full skirt, and tiny earrings. (*Wrong!* She should change the earrings to a larger shape to balance the skirt.)
2. She's wearing a two-piece print dress, leather belt with a medium-sized gold buckle, large gold earrings, and two small gold chains around her neck. (*Wrong!* She should use color to balance this look; beads in the background color of the print for the earrings and necklace would be good. The larger and more colorful the print, the larger the accessories should be.)
3. She's wearing a textured sweater vest, cotton skirt, and gold chain. (*Wrong!* With these nice textured fabrics, a mixture of beads and metals would be a better complement in jewelry.)

The proportions of the clothes you choose are affected by fashion cycles, because pieces that work together now may not have the proper proportions when you try mixing them with pieces you bought three years ago. To simplify your coping with the effects of changing fashion, I've developed a theory that describes the three major fashion cycles. The cycles are explained in Chapter 3, where you'll learn what proportions work together in each period.

To simplify your coping with the effects of changing fashion, I've developed a theory that describes the three major fashion cycles. The cycles are explained in Chapter 3.

What Do You Have in Mind?

Being well-groomed and well-dressed depends on your attitude as much as anything else. That attitude involves your mental image of yourself, a knowledge of what styles and colors become you, and a determination to plan a wardrobe that meets your every need. The person who makes excuses for a slip-shod appearance by saying, "If I had the money to spend on clothes that so-and-so does . . ." isn't fooling anyone. Without the proper attitude, it's entirely possible to spend a lot of money and still look dowdy and poorly groomed.

Look at it this way: If your hair is lank and badly styled, your skin dull, your nails uncared for, and your shoes unpolished, you will look poorly dressed in either a $29.95 special or a $1000 custom number. In your mental image of yourself, you must see yourself as neat; cleverly groomed with clean, shining hair, bright eyes, and healthy skin; having hands that look cared for; and wearing simple but becoming clothes and the best accessories you can afford.

Good grooming is a solid foundation for the development of self-confidence that leads to poise.

Good grooming is a solid foundation for the development of the self-confidence that leads to poise. Some people give the impression that they willfully let themselves get fat, neglect their hair and skin, and pick out any old thing when they shop for clothes. If they have nerve enough to look in a mirror, they must be as distressed as you are looking at them. But it's probably safe to assume that the impression they give of dressing without the aid of a mirror is literally true.

But in *your* case? Your whole approach to the day is improved by the feeling of well-being that good grooming brings you.

3.   The Three Cycles

The fashion industry has always represented itself with pride as being unpredictable. Each season breathless stories appear in *Vogue, Newsweek,* and our Sunday papers, telling us about the wonderful new directions designers in Paris, Rome, Tokyo, New York, and California are taking, and we see pictures of movie stars and international socialites watching fashion being unveiled on the runways of private design salons.

This excitement is designed to encourage all of us to shop—heaven forbid that you should be caught with wide lapels in a season of narrow lapels! Women who pride themselves on wearing the latest lines look in magazines and stores for signs and portents, and even women who have more modest fashion ambitions worry that skirt lengths will suddenly drop just when they've finally had their entire wardrobe shortened.

You may believe that after you've reviewed the new fashions, you will accept some new looks or reject others because they don't work for your figure. But why is it that what you bought two years ago now looks dated? Why doesn't your beautiful and formerly useful silk blouse work with the jacket you just bought? Why isn't your favorite skirt fun to wear anymore?

The truth is that it isn't just the details and fads of fashion that come and go, but entire wardrobe lines change.

The truth is that it isn't just the details and fads of fashion that come and go, but entire wardrobe lines change, and your perception of what looks good changes too, almost without your being aware of it. You've probably had the experience of suddenly realizing that all your pants looked awful because they were cut with terribly wide legs; you had to either reject them or have them all retailored to have the current narrower pants leg.

What if you could predict fashion changes? You could stop buying wide-legged pants before you got stuck with having perfectly good ones recut. You would know the difference between things that were at great sale prices because they were about to go out of fashion and things that are a genuine bargain because they will remain in style for several years.

In working with my clients as an image consultant, I have learned that most women do not have the time or inclination to really study fashion trends. They want to spend a minimum amount of time buying good-looking clothes for a minimum amount of money. I have been able to achieve this for them with my theory of the Three Cycles, and there's no reason you shouldn't put it to work for *you* too.

When I first began to study fashion, I noticed that, although fabrics and technology have changed considerably over the years, three basic lines have repeated themselves, always in the same order, in a surprisingly predictable way over a very long time. I actually went back as far as the Eighteenth Century and still found the same cyclic pattern.

The difference is that the rate at which the cycles repeat themselves is accelerating in contemporary life. In the French Court, fashion lines remained stable for twenty to thirty years, which meant that some people lived their entire adult lives in one wardrobe cycle. In the United States in the Twenties there was no television to flash new looks into every living room, and cycles were still about eight to ten years long. Once TV was firmly established in our culture, about in the Sixties, the cycles settled down to be about five years long for each.

My research and subsequent consulting experience has shown that you can with considerable confidence predict the basic lines of the next of the three fashion cycles, and you can recognize exactly where you are in the current cycle of five years.

Obviously, this varies somewhat because of special factors: If you live in a major metropolitan area like New York, Chicago, Dallas, Houston, Los Angeles, or San Francisco, fashion cycles move more quickly and are about one, two, or even three years ahead of smaller cities and rural areas where people are less exposed to fashion changes, and a new cycle may not take hold in these areas until a few years after they've begun in the major cities.

Climate also influences the speed with which the cycle where you live arrives. In areas like California and the Southwest, where there are only two fashion seasons, spring and fall, people tend to shop only when the season changes; and if they shop well, most of their clothes can be worn year-round. In the rest of

The rate at which the cycles repeat themselves is accelerating in contemporary life.

You can with considerable confidence predict the basic lines of the next fashion cycle.

the country, people must shop for four seasons, and because they're in the stores more often, they will more quickly see line changes and be receptive to them.

How Cycles Work

Characteristics that define each cycle mainly concern *line*—you can identify specific lines in blazers, skirts, pants, and blouses that are dominant in each of the three cycles. For example, collars: In one cycle, pointed collars dominate; in another, shawl collars and collarless looks; and in the third, ruffled, rounded collars. This one detail affects all the other details: A ruffly, rounded collar does not work well with a blazer that has lapels with pointed notches. When I talk about a *cycle,* I'm referring to a set of line characteristics that together are the major look of a five-year period.

When I talk about a cycle, I'm referring to a set of line characteristics that together are the major look of a five-year period.

Here's what you can expect to happen during each five-year cycle. In the first year, manufacturers and designers spark our interest in new lines by offering high-quality pieces at low prices. If you find a jacket that's very different from what you have at home, with a cut that seems a bit far-out to you, you're much likelier to experiment with it if the price is good and the fabric and buttons are excellent quality.

At the same time, a lot of familiar clothes begin going on sale. Your first reaction will be to buy a lot of clothes on sale—it's your lucky year! Resist that impulse!

For example, 1984 was a transition year, and here is what you found in the stores: On one rack, a blouse with puffy sleeves and a slightly rounded collar, in an average quality of fabric, marked down to $25. On another rack, a blouse with set-in sleeves and a pointed collar in silk for $65. If your purchase was the $65 blouse, you had made a five-year investment; if it was the $25 blouse, you would have had a hard time finding skirts, pants, and jackets that looked right with it by early 1985.

When you know what lines to look for in the first year of a new cycle, you will nearly always get higher quality at a lower price. Clothes are also simple in detail during the first year; our eyes have to be gradually tuned in to the new shapes. These purchases will be wearable for the next five years, and they'll also retain their elegance and be easy to accessorize because they are simple in line and detail.

In the first year of a new cycle, you will get high quality at a low price.

In the second year of the cycle, you'll get quality that is equal to the price you pay; people are beginning to realize that the fashion line has changed because they've been exposed over and over in magazines, on television talk shows and soap operas, in stores, and on some of their forward-looking friends. Some of the first-year clothes that were slow to sell will now be marked down, and can be very good buys—but the dye lots will have changed for the new season, so you shouldn't buy anything that you have to buy matched pieces for later.

In the second year of the cycle, you'll get quality that is equal to the price you pay.

In the second as in each succeeding year, an increasing number of details are added: jackets that had one button and two pockets now have two buttons and three pockets, and so on. Also, in the second and in each succeeding year, prices increase as details are added, somewhat as follows:

47

1st year: $125, classic blazer, 1 button,
2 pockets

2nd year: $200, tailored blazer, 2 buttons,
3 pockets

3rd year: $250, pea jacket, 6 buttons,
4 pockets, wider lapels, piping

4th year: $300, unstructured blazer with leather
shoulders and sleeves, fabric bodice
and lapels, unlined, different colors

5th year: $450, gold lamé jacket, unlined,
lots of detail

If you are still wearing the old lines in the second year of a cycle, you won't yet feel completely outdated because many other women are still resisting the new look too; you will notice that all of the fashion-visible women you know have moved on though. By the spring/summer shopping season, almost everyone will begin to experiment with the new lines because they are easy to find in the stores.

By the third year you will feel peer pressure to dress in the new line, and if you are just starting to buy, you will find that the quality is pretty low while prices are up—supply and demand in action. Elegant simplicity has pretty much vanished, and putting a flexible wardrobe together now is, therefore, much harder.

The cycle is reaching its peak, and designers and manufacturers have fun with all the ways to vary and experiment with the lines—amusing variations and fads turn up in the third year.

What may have looked like a drastic change to you at the beginning of the cycle has now become the standard fashion; designer looks are now being "knocked off" by manufacturers who sell to lower-priced and discount stores.

Prices skyrocket, and what started out as a simple, elegant line change becomes almost unrecognizable both in detail and fabric combination. The lines are now easily found everywhere and are worn by nearly everyone. During the fourth and fifth years, some of the transition clothes that are clues to the beginning of the next cycle now start to appear to train the eye to accept the coming changes.

This is the most difficult time for consumers: Clothes are dramatic and very detailed, they are mixed with puzzling transitional garments on the racks, and fads abound. Knickers, jumpsuits, and bell-bottom pants are all looks that tend to turn up during this confusing period.

If you purchased a well-planned wardrobe during the first and second year of the cycle, you can now afford to have fun with a fad or two. When I work with new clients with limited budgets who are just starting to buy the cycle's look in the third and fourth year, I suggest that they keep their purchases to a bare minimum and wait for the next cycle to be introduced. They can then invest in elegant, simple first-year clothes that will give them the best return on their wardrobe budget.

Accessories are wonderful items to buy to update your look during this late part of the cycle. A new belt or pair of shoes or necklace can refresh your familiar, well-planned wardrobe while you're waiting for the next cycle to begin. Those simple first and

By the third year of a new cycle, what looked like a dramatic change has now become the standard fashion.

During the fourth and fifth years, some of the transition clothes that are clues to the beginning of the next cycle now start to appear.

49

second year garments are easy to accessorize later on—another payoff for your good planning.

Let's review the shopping implications for the five-year cycle: My clients spend the bulk of their wardrobe money during the first and second year of the cycle, buying all the basic pieces for an entire wardrobe in the new line. In the third year they add a few pieces of jewelry, replace some blouses and shoes, and perhaps add to their evening wardrobe. In the fourth and fifth year they buy little or nothing while looking for the clues that will introduce the next five-year cycle. They may have fun with a fad or unusual accessory while they save their money for the beginning of the next cycle.

How to Recognize Clues to the Next Cycle

Evening wear is always one of the first ways new lines are brought onto the fashion scene.

There are many signals that the trained eye recognizes as indications of the changes to come. Evening wear is always one of the first ways new lines are brought onto the fashion scene. We're more conservative before 6:00 p.m. than after—candlelight makes us braver about trying new things. The fashion industry often introduces new lines around Christmas when the most shopping for evening wear is done. Often the latest evening look will evolve into a toned-down daytime version.

Color often announces design changes. I've noticed that black velvet in particular is often used to introduce new lines—probably because all women, even

those who never wear black, find its elegance irresist-
ible and always look at it in the stores. It may be used,
for example, in the form of black velveteen collars and
cuffs on suit jackets and coats, or as piping on skirt
waistlines or blazers, spotlighting the very area that is
changing so that shoppers can't miss the new look.
White is another color that is used on collars or piping
to point out line changes.

*Color is often
used to spotlight
the very area
where the line
is changing.*

These accents disappear in midcycle when everyone understands the lines, then reappear during the
transition period. This doesn't mean that you can't
continue to wear these garments with contrasting
details—you just won't find them for sale anymore. If
you purchased the right variation of the line, you can
wear it for the entire five-year period.

Accessories also offer clues: If necklaces are getting
bolder and more colorful, it often means that fabrics
will be more colorful and that the shape of garments
will also be more bold in line, requiring strong jewelry.
If you see lots of high heels, that tells you that longer,
fuller skirts will be a major line. If you see lots of
handbags with handles instead of shoulderbags,
watch for round, ruffled collars and puffy sleeves
that shoulderstraps wouldn't work with.

Transitional periods have many traps for the un-
wary. For example, if we are moving from a cycle
that has round collars to one that has pointed
collars, manufacturers may provide a transitional
jacket that has a lapel with half of its notch rounded
and half pointed. The idea is to get you used to the
pointedness to come, but allow you to continue to
wear your round-collared blouses. Once the new cycle
is established, however, the blouses with pointed col-

lars won't work with this jacket, and it will turn out to be a poor purchase.

Retailers have trouble during this period, too, especially in this area of matching collars between blouses and jackets. Mannekins in store windows often wear unfortunate combinations—a blouse with a new pointed collar shown with a jacket that has rounded notches; a shawl-collared blouse worn beneath a notched lapel. Customers are often confused, and unlikely to be critical of these errors.

Now that you know how five-year cycles work, you're ready to be introduced to the lines that characterize each one of them. I call them the *Town and Country Cycle, Sophisticate Cycle,* and *Gamin Cycle.* Keep in mind that they repeat in that order every fifteen years. As you read, you should refer to the summary charts on pages 78 and 79 so that you can see most clearly how the three cycles contrast.

The Town and Country Cycle

The most important characteristic of the Town and Country Cycle is that during the entire cycle the emphasis is on *separates*. In stores you'll see blouses, blazers, jackets, sweaters, vests, skirts, pants, and dresses—all presented separately and intended to be combined in many ways.

During the entire Town and Country Cycle, the emphasis is on separates.

A typical Town and Country Cycle combination would be a white blouse, navy blazer, and gray skirt: You see three totally separate pieces combined to create one look.

This cycle started on the East Coast in about 1983 and on the West Coast in 1984.

Layering

The second important characteristic of this style is *layering*. Since you are working with many separate pieces, designers naturally put them together to create a layered look. Even dresses become layered; for example, a dress might appear to have two blouses, a vest, a jacket, and a skirt, when in fact it is three pieces of fabric made to look like two blouses and a vest, stitched to a skirt, with a separate jacket added—all in different colors to give the appearance of layered separates. This dress treatment shows up only during the Town and Country Cycle.

The second important characteristic of this style is layering.

A typical layering technique is a jacket over a vest, over a shirt, over a turtleneck sweater. You'll see this throughout the cycle, beginning with a jacket and vest over a blouse; each year the layering becomes more exaggerated, until the blouse has a vest and the jacket has another vest. When this double vesting

53

appears, you know that the Town and Country Cycle is almost over.

The H-Shape

The *H-shape* is the overall line during the Town and Country Cycle. You will notice that when these separates are put together, the emphasis is on the shoulders and hips, creating a rectangular shape centered at the waist. These clothes are a natural fit for women with an H-shaped body; see Chapter 2 to review how your body will fit this fashion line.

Line Detail

The Town and Country Cycle, like all the cycles, is best defined in terms of line detail. Below I will describe how each type of garment will look during this cycle.

Blouses   Blouses have pointed or highly tailored collars with set-in sleeves and a seam across the shoulder. As the cycle progresses, this shoulder seam evolves into an epaulet—a detail found only in the Town and Country Cycle. Another typical blouse has a dolman or dropped-sleeve design with a turtleneck or cowl neck.

Blazers and Jackets   Blazers and jackets have notched, widely spread lapels, with definite points at the end of each notch. At the beginning of the cycle the notches are about an inch wide, but they open up as the lapel increases in size during the cycle. Exaggeration of lapels and lapel notches is evident by the third year, and becomes positively humorous in some designs by the fifth year. Jackets have set-in dropped sleeves, and can be single- or double-breasted. Double-breasted blazers will tend to be sold with pants, while single-breasted jackets are sold with skirts. You know that the Town and Country Cycle is well established when you see more blazers than suit jackets on store racks.

During the Town and Country Cycle, blazers and jackets have notched, widely spaced lapels, with definite points at the end of each notch.

Sweaters   Sweaters of all types are very important to the Town and Country Cycle. The most common sweater is the blazer sweater with notched lapels, single- or double-breasted, and with a set-in sleeve. There are a lot of sweater vests, turtlenecks, cowl necks, cardigans with matching pullovers, and unusual sweaters with dolman or dropped sleeves. Sweater dresses with sweater vests or sweater jackets are also prolific. You will find suits consisting of a wool gabardine skirt with a textured sweater jacket, a combination common to the Town and Country Cycle but rare in either of the other cycles.

55

Vests Vests are really only seen much during the Town and Country Cycle. The most classic form is the button-front vest with a belt across the back, which is worn under a suit jacket or blazer. As the cycle progresses, you see vests in all imaginable shapes, sizes, and fabric combinations. Toward the end of the cycle you'll be glad to know that it will disappear for another ten years!

Skirts Skirts during this cycle are typically A-line (circle skirts and wraparound), the pant skirt with a fly-front zipper and belt loops sewn onto the waistband, and box-pleated with each pleat perfectly square. During this cycle you often see the return of the mini-skirt—the only Town and Country characteristic that men will be happy about.

Pants Pants during the Town and Country Cycle have fly-front zippers, belt loops sewn onto the waistband, and a dart on either side of the zipper. Side zippers appear only at the beginning of the cycle in the simpler, more elegant first-year garments, and are usually hidden inside the left pocket. As the cycle starts out, pants will have wider legs with cuffs to accentuate the change in width; by the second and third years, the cuff will be dropped, and by the end of the cycle the width will be exaggerated as bell-bottom pants. For evening wear, wide-legged pajama pants will be fashionable.

Pants tend to dominate the Town and Country Cycle because skirts so often become quite short. Women who don't feel comfortable in miniskirts tend to choose a pant suit look rather than a skirt suit.

Dresses   Dresses have three major shapes during this cycle. The most typical is the shirtdress with a pointed collar, set-in or dropped sleeve, an A-line skirt, and front buttons either all the way to the hem or down to the waist; a narrow belt is worn with the shirtwaist. A second shape is the a layered look described earlier, often with the shape of the shirtdress, but with a blouse of one color sewn to a skirt of another color, and with a belt of still another color. Finally, this is the cycle for coat dresses. They are shaped exactly like a coat, can be either single- or double-breasted, and have a pointed collar with notched lapels, and set-in sleeves. The coat dress sometimes has a belt and sometimes is worn straight.

57

Coats Coats during the Town and Country Cycle have two basic shapes. The trenchcoat has a notched collar with set-in sleeves, epaulets at the shoulder and sleeve cuff, and is either single- or double-breasted. The alternate coat has a wide, notched collar and set-in sleeves, and is also either single- or double-breasted. It has both long and skirt-length styles, as well as a short car coat or tunic length. It is most frequently sold in heavy wools. Classic coat colors in this cycle are camel and navy.

Accessories Accessories during the Town and Country Cycle tend to be small, because the complexity of combining all those separates doesn't leave a lot of room for accessories that make a strong statement.

Jewelry features loop earrings, chains, charm bracelets and necklaces, lapel pins, and tailored watches. Rings on each finger become popular toward the end of the cycle because clothes don't have much room for other accessories. The most commonly used metals are silver, white gold, and platinum, which blend best with the grayed color tones of the cycle, which I'll discuss in the next section.

Scarves are very popular—you'll see everything from tie scarves for tailored blouses, to large squares and shawls to wear over dresses and skirts. Scarves are very workable with all the layered of separates and pointed collars that are typical of Town and Country.

Belts become narrower to fit into the belt loops that are sewn onto the skirts' and pants' waistbands, and for the same reason they'll be straight rather than shaped belts. Again because of the grayed tones of the cycle, silver buckles are common. At the beginning of the cycle you'll see double-wrapped belts with the look of two narrow belts worn together; this evolves into a single narrow belt.

Shoes are either open- or closed-toe pumps, but in either case the toe area is pointed. In the middle of the cycle, platform shoes appear because of the dominance of pants, which are assumed to look best with higher heels. Heels will often be stacked or wooden, and will tend to be squarer in nearly every type of shoe. Oxfords are popular, both low ones for pants and casual wear and heeled versions to be worn with pants and plaid or pleated skirts.

Stockings are natural-colored for the most tailored looks, but opaque colored stockings are also popular, with the commonest colors being black, navy, white, burgundy, and green. You can achieve the same balance that boots give by wearing opaque stockings and pumps in an exactly identical color. Because of the popularity of pants and oxford shoes, knee socks will return in all lengths, shapes, and color combinations.

Handbags will generally be shoulder-strap bags. If you're the sort of person who likes to carry your tennis shoes, your lunch, your baby's diapers, your wallet, photo album, and all your makeup—you'll *love* Town and Country purses, because they have a generous size and the shoulder strap makes them easy to carry. Even briefcases come with shoulder straps.

Studding and beading are often used during the Town and Country Cycle, probably because it adds interest in a cycle that is difficult to accessorize. Usually you see beading in the winter months and studding in spring and summer. Town and Country evening wear includes a lot of beading with sequins or studding done in silver.

Color

Almost all of the color tones used during the Town and Country Cycle are grayed in tone (which is why jewelry and belt buckles in silver work so well). This gray undertone takes practice to recognize, but the trained eye can see it everywhere, even in the shades of black that are used.

As with all three cycles, the new lines are introduced in black, but by the end of the first year, when consumers are aware of the line changes, navy replaces black. The basic Town and Country colors are navy, brown, camel, gray, true red, and white; with red, white, and blue as a classic color combination that is emphasized in the spring collections of the first year of the cycle.

Other common Town and Country colors are rust, warm brown, moss and kelly greens, lemon yellow, pink, peach, and all shades of blue.

The basic Town and Country colors are navy, brown, camel, gray, true red, and white— almost all are grayed in tone.

Summary

To summarize, the five-year Town and Country Cycle is characterized by the use of separates that are layered with increasing complexity as the cycle progresses. The overall line has an H-shape, with emphasis on shoulders and hips. Although scarves can be mixed with separates well, jewelry is less creative than during other cycles because it would otherwise add too much complexity to an already complex look. Colors are shown in grayed tones, with the primary colors being the classic "preppie" colors of navy, brown, camel, gray, true red, and white.

The Sophisticate Cycle

The most notable characteristics of the Sophisticate Cycle are the use of solids and the simplicity of lines used in garments throughout the five-year cycle. When we say a woman is sophisticated, we mean that she is refined, worldly wise, and elegantly put together; and this effect is best accomplished without the cuteness of prints and the fun of detailed lines.

There are *some* prints to be found during the Sophisticate Cycle, but you have to look long and hard to find them. If you stand in the middle of a store during this cycle, you'll be overwhelmed by the number of solid colors you see, and the clothes around you will give you a feeling of elegance and simplicity.

The Y-Shape

The shape of clothing during the Sophisticate Cycle is that of a Y. Emphasis is on the shoulders, and shoulder pads become standard in blouses and jackets. There are lots of straight skirts and wide-shouldered, belted jackets for the effect of a Y-shape.

Line Detail

The simplicity of line detail could be called classic, or even severe. You will notice that designers put a great deal of emphasis on craftsmanship and the "finish" of clothes; everyone seems to be trying to outdo everyone else with a rich look. Below are the line details typical of the Sophisticate Cycle.

Blouses Blouses have oval or shawl-collared necklines, providing excellent space for accessories. The shawl collar is the most typical collar shape, and sleeves are set-in or raglan. Buttons are hidden by a fold of fabric down the front of blouses, providing a beautiful simplicity.

Blazers and Jackets Blazers and jackets are very much featured because of the emphasis on shoulders. Suits are built around their jackets, and jackets have the same oval or shawl-collared necklines that blouses have. As with blouses, the sleeves are set-in or raglan, and there is often a button at the wrist to make the sleeve more tapered. Jackets are usually belted, often with the belt attached to the jacket and in the same fabric. This sometimes creates a peplum effect—the look of a little skirt below the waist, ending at the hip bone. Jackets are often short, ending at or above the hip bone.

During the Sophisticate Cycle, suits are built around their jackets, and jackets have the same oval or shawl-collared necklines that blouses have.

Blazers, like jackets, are short, often have three buttons, and have set-in sleeves. Lapels are quite narrow, with notches that are also narrow, creating a shawl-collared effect. Sophisticate Cycle blazers are quite classic, but even some blazers have an attached belt. Pockets are usually inset with

63

only the flap showing, or even missing altogether, especially on belted blazers.

Sweaters Sweaters are usually pullover with a fitted waist and peplum effect. Even those that do not have separate belts have a belted effect. Sweaters that open in the front have shawl collars and raglan sleeves, and are always belted.

Skirts Skirts in the Sophisticate Cycle always appear to be straight. Waist-bands are an inch to an inch and a half in width and have no belt loops. If there is any gathering, it is usually on only the front or back of the skirt. Nearly every skirt during this cycle has a slit. Slits begin as a single slit or pleat in back, then show in nearly every possible position as the cycle progresses: one on each side in the front, off-center in the front, or one in front and one in back. Toward the end of the cycle the slits become much deeper and more daring.

Pants Pants become fuller at the hipline and fall gently all the way to the ankle, narrowing as they go. I like to compare pants legs during this

cycle to the sleeves—they both get
narrower at the bottom for a sort
of raglan effect. Pants legs are sometimes anchored at the bottom by
a button or elastic at the ankle bone,
which at its most exaggerated gives
a harem pants look that is especially
popular for evening wear. Pants'
zippers are generally in the back.

Dresses Dresses have collarless, oval necklines
or shawl collars during the Sophisticate Cycle. Sleeves are set-in or
raglan, and buttons are usually
hidden under a fold of fabric. Like
skirts, dresses often have slits in the
skirt, usually one on either side.
The skirt line is straight, with a
tailored waistline that has an attached
belt. Simple, all-one-color silk dresses
are very popular during the cycle.

Coats Coats are in wrapped styles, in many
cases without buttons altogether.
Sleeves are set-in or raglan, and
the shape is narrow and straight
down to the hem. Collars are shawl
or collarless, or in some cases a plain
stand-up collar. Fur collars are often
attached to Sophisticate coats, giving
a rounded effect and often covering
a fabric shawl collar underneath.

Accessories   Accessories are very important during the Sophisticate Cycle, because the simplicity of garments lends itself so well to accessorizing.

Jewelry is elegant, with metals in yellow gold and yellowish brass, with the yellow deepening as the cycle progresses, and there is a liberal use of pearls and dressy stones. Earrings are large, dangling loops or diamond or button shapes; gold surrounding a pearl is a beautiful earring found in this cycle. Strings of pearls are worn with everything, and you'll need to own them in all lengths. Garnets, gold beads, and even the plastic beads worn with summer clothes are small and round like pearls. Rhinestones and diamond-like pins that would be considered too dressy for daytime wear in other cycles are used now on suits and dresses, and look perfectly appropriate on the Sophisticate Cycle's simple, elegant clothes.

Scarves all but disappear during this cycle. Toward the end of the Sophisticate Cycle you'll briefly see some large square shawls, usually worn over the shoulder and tucked into the belt at the waist.

Belts are a vital accessory during the Sophisticate Cycle, and you can't have too many of them. They'll come in all widths and descriptions, and you'll wear them over jackets, blazers, sweaters, and blouses. Garments often come with matching fabric belts, and you will be able to change their look by using an alternate belt. Belt buckles are elegant, and metals are usually gold-toned.

Shoes often have anklestraps during this cycle, and lots of strappy, heeled sandals appear, to flatter legs revealed by slit skirts or to add height with the flowing pants lines. Toes are rounded or squared, and heels are high and somewhat rectangular. Elegance reigns supreme, with lots of suede in the winter and patent leather in the spring and summer, and open-toed shoes are popular year-round.

Boots are not very useful because of the slit skirts, although short boots that blend well with pants are good, and with the correct stocking they can complement some of the skirts. In bad weather, women during the Sophisticate Cycle often wear boots outside, then take them off when they are inside again—switching to their anklestrap shoes.

Stockings are generally natural-colored, since slit skirts feature legs so flatteringly—you don't want your legs to blend with your clothes. For evening, sheer black stockings with a seam in back are occasionally seen, and this is just about the only whimsy around during the Sophisticate Cycle.

Handbags match shoes exactly during this cycle, in whatever fabric or color. The envelope shape is very popular, generally in a large or small rectangle. Shoulder straps are too casual for the Sophisticate Cycle's elegant clothes, and handled purses reappear. Briefcases generally have handles and are often in elegant textures like suede or snakeskin.

Color

Sophisticate Cycle colors are very severe: the most common are black, ivory, and burgundy. All other colors are quite intense.

Sophisticate Cycle colors are very severe: the most common are black, ivory, and burgundy. All other colors are quite intense—for example, royal blue, magenta, fuchsia, royal purple, taupe, and bright red. Metal colors are gold or yellow brass, becoming a deeper yellow as the cycle evolves.

Summary

To summarize, the Sophisticate Cycle uses almost all solids in rather severe and intense colors. The line is a T-shape, with wide shoulders and straight garments. Everything is simple, rich, and elegant—by far the dressiest of the cycles, even for daytime wear.

The Gamin Cycle

The French word *gamin* means "a young girl with saucy charm." I chose the name Gamin for this cycle because its clothes convey a young and girlish mood. I have to confess that this is my favorite cycle because its clothes are friendly and fun to wear.

The most important characteristic of the cycle is the use of prints, and by this I mean anything that's not a solid color: prints include stripes, tweeds, textured fabrics like raw silk, and fabrics with woven patterns all in the same color. If you stand in the middle of a store at the height of the Gamin Cycle, you'll be overwhelmed by all the prints around you, and by the third year you'll have a hard time finding any solids except for those with a tone-on-tone design incorporated in the fabric.

The most important characteristic of the cycle is the use of prints, and by this I mean anything that's not a solid color.

The 8-Shape

The Gamin Cycle line is very rounded with lots of emphasis on the waist. This creates an 8-shape, or snowman shape. Sleeves are puffy and full, skirts are gathered and full—there's a real emphasis on the female body. To see how your figure shape coordinates with clothes during this cycle, refer to Chapter 2.

Line Detail

There are lots of interesting line details and combinations of details in the structure of each Gamin Cycle garment. In fact, it's this very trait that keeps many women from responding quickly to this cycle. Because of the wealth of prints and details, a woman who prides herself on wearing classic and very tailored clothes will initially believe that these new lines are just fads. The danger is that by the time her eye has adjusted to the subtler forms of Gamin garments, the simpler garments of the first year or two will no longer be available because the cycle will already have progressed to more detailed and flamboyant designs.

Here are some of the specifics of Gamin Cycle line detail.

Blouses Blouses of all types have rounded collars—even tailored versions. Collars are pleated, peter pan, gathered, or ruffled. If a blouse has an attached tie, it is narrow and attached to a narrow band at the collar area. Sometimes more than one tie is attached.

Sleeve detail is also important: They'll be puffy or gathered or pleated at the shoulder; sometimes they'll be full and puffy at the top, then taper slightly from the elbow to the wrist. In the summer, many blouses have puffy sleeves that end in a narrow cuff or band of elastic just above the elbow.

Blazers and Jackets Blazers and jackets have narrow lapels with notches that are often rounded— the notches vary widely and are an area of great creativity for designers during this cycle. You'll find triangular notches, rectangular notches, three notches to a lapel, and toward the end of the cycle, an ambiguous form that combines rounding above the notch and a point below.

All blazers and jackets have puffy or gathered or pleated detail at the shoulders, and they're short and somewhat fitted to the body. Buttons are small and you'll have a lot of them.

Blazers and jackets have narrow lapels with notches that are often rounded . . . and have puffy or gathered or pleated detail at the shoulders.

Sweaters Sweaters have rounded, often textured collars like lace, with sleeves that are of course puffy, gathered, or pleated at the shoulder. This cycle provides lots of interesting textures in sweaters—for example, angora and ribbons knitted together to create a "print." Most Gamin Cycle sweaters are colorful and ruffly and many pull on over the head.

Skirts Skirts are often gathered all around the waist and attached to a narrow waistband; or gathered only at the front and back on a one-and-a-half-inch waistband; or pleated onto a very wide triangular-shaped waistband. You hear these skirts described variously as gathered, full, or dirndl skirts. If Gamin Cycle skirts have pleats, they'll be knife pleats that begin at the waistband and continue to the hemline.

A sure sign of a Gamin Cycle garment is a flounce at the bottom of a skirt. At the beginning of the cycle this is a delicate detail, but by the third year, flounces may begin at the hipline and repeat all the way to the hemline. By the fourth and fifth years, you'll find lacy petticoats hanging below ruffled skirts to create a very flouncy appearance indeed.

Pants   Pants are similar to skirts, with lots of pleating and gathering at the waistline. Because of this, zippers or closure areas tend to be at the side or back of pants. Waistbands are often two to three inches wide all the way around, or may show variations such as the obi effect—wide in front, narrowing on the sides, and wide again in back; or triangular in front, pointing down, and narrowing toward the sides and back.

Pants legs, because of all that fabric at the waist, are wide at the hips, then begin narrowing as the leg goes down. They appear to be wide on top and narrow at the bottom, and end at or above the ankle bone.

At the beginning of the cycle, pants typically have three or four pleats on each side. In the third year, these pleats begin to be stitched down. By the fourth year there are only two stitched-down pleats and the waistband is getting narrower. The fifth year starts to take on Town and Country characteristics: narrow waistband, fly-front zipper, and belt loops.

Dresses Dresses are very popular now—you could almost call Gamin Cycle a dress cycle. There are lots of matching patterned skirts and blouses that together have the look of a dress. Dresses have all the Gamin characteristics: round, ruffly, or peter pan collars; sleeves that are puffy, gathered, or pleated at the shoulder; and skirts that are gathered, often on an elastic waistband. Dresses are full in shape, and have lots of unusual sleeve and neckline detail.

Coats Coats resemble jackets, with rounded or stand-up ruffled collars. Sleeves are puffy, gathered, or pleated at the shoulder-line, and the overall line is fitted at the bodice with fullness

in the skirt area. Because of all the
unusual sleeve and collar detail, many
cape styles are shown—a style unique
to the Gamin Cycle.

Accessories Accessories during the Gamin Cycle
are colorful and whimsical and bold,
to balance all the prints.

Jewelry is larger than during the
other two cycles, and round shapes
predominate. Necklaces are colorful
with lots of round beads and big, bold
shapes. Earrings are also quite big
and button-shaped. Pins are rather
romantic brooches, and rings are of
unusual design and rounded shapes.
Wrist watches tend to be round or oval
and sometimes have colorful faces.
Commonly used materials for jewelry
are garnets, pearls, and colorful
stones of all kinds. Metals are bronze
and brass, with the yellow gold of
the last cycle still popular but
beginning to be combined with silver.
An example would be an earring with
a yellow gold background and a white
gold foreground.

Scarves are usually long and narrow
as opposed to the squares of other
cycles. Ribbons and ties are much
more commonly used than scarves,
which are mostly used for special

effects, like using a long narrow scarf to tie a rose around the neck for a romantic effect.

Belts are a necessity in your wardrobe during the Gamin Cycle because of all the heavily gathered and pleated skirts and sleeves—it's necessary to give the waist a narrower accent. This is not only more flattering to the figure, but necessary for the 8-shape line of the cycle. Belts are very wide— from one to five inches wide, in fact. They come in all shapes and there is a wealth of wonderful, very creative belt buckles.

Shoes have rounded toes, and even the part at the base of the arch will be rounded. At the beginning of the cycle, both high heels and low heels are used, but as the cycle progresses, lower heels predominate because they create a better proportion with the cycle's full garments. The heels themselves tend to be round or pointed, and are often thicker at the top and very thin at the bottom. Gamin Cycle shoes include many interesting fabrics and textures, and solid shoes are sometimes hard to find because designers are putting colorful combinations together to complement the clothes.

Boots are not essential during the Gamin Cycle, but they are often used with flounced skirts. Boots tend to be shorter and to have a Western or ethnic look.

Stockings are a very important accent during Gamin Cycle. Your clothes call for opaque stockings in every color you wear—white, ivory, gray, black, blue, red, green, yellow, pink. . . . White and ivory stockings are appropriate for every season during the entire cycle. Men rarely like colored stockings, especially during the day, but natural-colored stockings are almost never worn during this cycle. The only time I suggest you wear natural stockings is when you want to keep a special man happy or when your specific career dictates that you need to be conservative.

Handbags are mostly handled or wrist-strap clutch. All purses are smaller and tend to be rounded in shape. If you prefer shoulder-strap purses, you'll find that they don't work very well with the heavy detail on the shoulders and sleeves of your clothes. You'll be able to buy shoulder-strap handbags, but I wouldn't advise it; if you need a larger size, carry a briefcase.

Color

The Gamin Cycle is unique in its use of color. Almost no attention is paid to the basic or neutral colors that are useful in the other two cycles, and all colors tend to have a bronze undertone. For example, red is an orange-red, green becomes olive, white becomes oyster, beige becomes bronze, yellow becomes mustard, and blue becomes teal, and gold metals look like a combination of copper and brass.

During this cycle, even belt buckles, buttons, clasps, and other metal items have a brassy or bronzed effect that coordinates perfectly with the colors used in solid as well as printed fabrics.

During the Gamin Cycle, almost no attention is paid to the basic or neutral colors that are useful in the other two cycles, and all colors tend to have a bronze undertone.

Summary

The Gamin Cycle is a cycle of prints and playful, detailed looks. The clothes have an 8-shape, with full skirts and sleeves that are puffy at the shoulder. Wide belts that accent the waist complete the proportion. Colors are bright and have a brassy undertone, and jewelry is colorful and large to balance the heavy use of bright patterns and full lines.

(The table and illustrations on the next two pages summarize the line differences between The Three Cycles.)

The Three Cycles

Town &
Country
Cycle

Pointed, notched collar
Set-in, shoulder seams
Patch pockets
Textured blazer

Sophisticate
Cycle

Shawl collar
Set-in, shoulder seams
Set-in pockets
Solid fabrics
Belted jackets

Gamin
Cycle

Rounded, notched lapels
Pleated, gathered
shoulder seams
No pockets
Printed fabrics
Open jackets

The Three Cycles

	TOWN AND COUNTRY	SOPHISTICATE	GAMIN
Emphasis	Separates	Solids	Prints
Line	Pointed or square lines	Oval or rectangular lines	Rounded lines
Shape	H-shaped	T-shaped	8-shaped
Collars	Pointed, tailored, notched	Shawl, collarless	Rounded, puffy
Sleeves	Set-in, shoulder seam, dolman	Set-in, raglan	Puffy, pleated, or gathered
Lapels	Wide notches, pointed notches	Shawls, narrow, or lapelless	Rounded notches, narrow notches
Skirts	Front-fly-skirt, wrap skirt A-line, box pleats	Straight, slit, side or back zipper	Full, gathered, dirndl, flounced, knife pleats
Shoes	Pointed toes, platform and stacked heels	Pumps, ankle straps, high heels	Rounded toes, medium to low heels
Colors	Grayed colors	Clear colors	Bronzed colors
Metals	Silver/gold combined White gold Platinum	Yellow gold Yellowish brass	Copper Bronzed brass
Bead Shapes	Oblong Rectangular	Small, round Diamond-shaped	Large, round

How Fashion Cycles Happen

If you are like most of my clients, hearing about these cycles for the first time, you may find it hard to believe that the confusing changes in fashion are as predictable as a series of three five-year cycles. It sounds as if all the fashion designers and manufacturers would have to do is to sit down in a room and agree on what direction to take next, and then agree on how to get consumers to accept the changes.

Each new cycle is a reaction against the style of each preceding cycle.

The truth is, though, that each new cycle is a reaction against the style of each preceding cycle. For example, during the Sophisticate Cycle, when everyone is wearing elegant, simple clothes in austere neutral colors, both designers and consumers will naturally begin craving the fun of patterns and bright colors of the Gamin Cycle is a response to this.

As the Gamin Cycle hits its height with ruffles over ruffles over eyelet, the mind starts craving tailored looks, but people are not ready to give up patterns altogether, so the tailored Town and Country mixture of solid and patterned separates is a natural evolution. Eventually, all those Town and Country separates and layered looks, not to mention the cycle's casualness, call for a reaction of simplicity and elegance, and the Sophisticate Cycle is with us once again.

The media is largely responsible for helping the cycles along—I find that talk shows and soap operas are the best ways to track fashion changes. Boutiques and department stores often donate clothes to celebrities and soap operas in order to keep people interested in fashion change. Watching these new clothes on television can help your eye become accustomed to the new lines and give you early clues to trends in wardrobe, makeup, and hairstyles.

It is important to distinguish between fads and genuine fashion changes. If you thoroughly understand the three natural fashion cycles I've described, you will be helped enormously in this.

Fads are often useful, however, for showing us new looks so that we can familiarize our eyes with the new proportions. They usually occur during the fourth and fifth year of a cycle and combine dominant characteristics of the current cycle with a line from the next.

For example, pants dominate during the Town and Country Cycle, and toward the end of the cycle culottes appear—so we can stay in pants while getting used to seeing ourselves in the skirts that dominate the Sophisticate Cycle that's coming next. Or, at the end of the Gamin Cycle you'll see jumpsuits on the racks—they keep the dominant 8-shape but get us used to the blouson jackets and pants that will be so popular in the Town and Country Cycle. Another end-of-Gamin-Cycle fad is the dropped-waist dress, which leads the eye into the tunics and skirts of the Town and Country Cycle.

Most of these fads turn up first in the junior departments of stores, and can also be found in evening or designer wear. At best, fads last only about two years, so they are not a good investment if you are on a tight wardrobe budget, or saving for the first year of the next cycle. On the other hand, if you invested wisely in the first year or two of the current cycle, you may be willing to splurge on something fun that will only work for two years.

Investing in Five-Year Cycles

Remember the formula I introduced at the beginning of this chapter: You should spend the most clothing money in the first year of a new cycle, buying the simpler, higher-quality garments that designers use to introduce a new line. Make sure that you purchase all items in a given color within six months, because the dye lots change each season and you will have a hard time matching things after that.

In the second year you can add some complementary clothes at a modest investment, but for the remaining three years you should not have to buy anything but replacements for blouses and shoes, or additional accessories that give your clothes fresh new looks. If your budget is limited, you should begin saving for the first year of the next cycle.

Most women buy a blouse here, a skirt there, a pair of shoes somewhere else—with no idea of whether they will work in their wardrobe over a period of several years. If, at the end of the Gamin Cycle, you don't realize that the clothes will shortly be tailored, you will probably continue to buy ruffly blouses with collars and sleeves that won't work with any jackets you buy a year later. Sale racks will be particularly seductive during these transition periods, with a wealth of merchandise marked down drastically.

You may think of a blouse as a low-cost purchase, or as something you should never spend a lot of money on. But buying inexpensively is not necessarily the best way to invest in your wardrobe. Will that

$35 blouse work with anything in two years? Does it only go with one skirt? Or six different things? An $80 blouse that will work with many pieces in your wardrobe and that will last for the next three to five years is a far better investment than a $35 blouse that has a short life. Single-item mistakes, however individually low in cost, can quickly add up to a lot of badly spent wardrobe money.

Single-item mistakes, however individually low in cost, can quickly add up to a lot of badly spent wardrobe money.

At first, working with the five-year cycle will seem expensive to you, because it means buying a lot of clothes at once the first year of a new cycle. But once you have gone through a whole cycle and discovered how much you enjoyed your clothes and how well they worked together for the entire five years, you'll never go back to buying bits and pieces again.

4. The Seven Looks

Suppose that when you got up in the morning, you could think about what you were going to be doing that day, and could choose clothes that would make the day go more smoothly and help you succeed in your day's goals? You *can!*

I have identified seven ways that you can put your wardrobe together for seven different moods, and if you master this part of my wardrobe strategy, you will not only have a more flexible clothing investment, but you will have help in achieving your daily interpersonal goals.

Most people do not believe that what they wear affects the people around them very much; sometimes they know they look pretty or elegant, and they notice that some clothes seem to attract compliments from other people. But clothes function at a subconscious level as well, and men and women and children may react to clothes in entirely different ways.

Men, women, and children react to clothes in different ways.

Some ways of combining your clothes convey power and self-confidence, while others make people feel comfortable with you and give them the impression that you're a friendly person. Most people dress around a single image—a career woman might want to convey power and credibility, for example, or a mother might always dress to make other people comfortable.

But what happens when the businesswoman talks to her child's teacher at a PTA meeting—does she really want the teacher to be a little intimidated? The chances are that she won't hear the truth about problems her child is having, because the teacher will want to present herself as completely in control, just as the businesswoman appears to be. Or what about when the mother is running for president of the PTA —she needs to dress more powerfully in order to have the other parents perceive her as having leadership qualities.

You probably spend quite a bit of money on your clothes, and you should have fun with them.

You probably spend quite a bit of money on your clothes, and you should have fun with them. Unless you know how to change their effect by mixing them in new ways, you won't be getting the fun of experimentation and you won't be getting the maximum return on your investment.

Distinguishing Between Cycle and Look

The seven looks you can have are called the *Town and Country Look*, the *Sophisticate Look*, the *Gamin Look*, the *Romantic Look*, the *Patrician Look*, the *Exotic Look*, and the *Docent Look*. You'll notice that Town and Country, Sophisticate, and Gamin are also the names of the three cycles. I didn't do this just to confuse you, but because the looks and cycles that share names also share important qualities.

However, remember that *cycle* refers to line—a set of line characteristics that together are the major look of a five-year period; while *look* refers to the way clothes are combined to give a specific effect and convey a certain mood. All seven looks occur within each of the three cycles—a Romantic Look dress in the Gamin Cycle will have a round collar and puffy sleeves, a Romantic Look dress in the Town and Country Cycle will have a tailored lacy collar and set-in sleeves.

Cycle refers to line—while look refers to the way clothes are combined to give a specific effect and convey a certain mood.

I'm going to summarize each look for you, giving two examples and describing how women, men, and children respond to the look. You'll notice that all seven illustrations are in styles typical of the Town and Country Cycle—the current line in most of the United States.

The Town and Country Look

Characteristic   Tailored separates used in combination

Mood   Casual, sporty, conservative, suburban, mannish

How to Create This Look

A navy blazer worn with a white blouse and gray skirt is a conservative version of this look. A more casual version would be a tweed jacket worn over a sweater-vest and oxford-cloth shirt, with a solid-color or plaid wool skirt. Print fabrics are often used for one or more of the pieces. The outfit shown here is recognizably a Town and Country Cycle version because of its pointed collar, pointed notches on the blazer, and fly-front skirt zipper.

Where to Wear This Look

Because of the moods listed above, a person dressed in a Town and Country Look gives the impression of being a homebody with either a part-time or suburban career, and someone who enjoys outdoor activities on weekends. Some of the best places to wear this look would be at home, athletic events, suburban offices, schools and universities, volunteer organizations, women's clubs, country clubs, and various activities involving children.

How Women Respond to This Look

Retail stores use this look in most of their displays because it shows so many different pieces; therefore, women are used to it and respond to it very well. Its casual, suburban attitude is also appealing to women because it corresponds well with the lifestyle demands many of them have.

How Men Respond to This Look

Because of its slightly mannish mood, men respond to it well in business and casual situations, when the Town and Country Look seems to them to be a practical way to dress. Because men look at themselves so often in this look, they see it as reflecting their own masculine qualities, and you will probably not appeal to them as a woman—there isn't much femininity connected with this look.

How Children Respond to This Look

Children find the Town and Country Look comfortable to be around because it's casual and has an interesting blend of fabrics.

The Sophisticate Look

Characteristic   The use of a single solid color

Mood   Power, credibility, elegance,
independence, self-confidence

How to Create This Look

A good example of this look is a black wool dress
worn with black or natural stockings, black shoes, and
a black belt, accented only with gold necklace and
earrings. Metals like gold and silver do not count as a
second color. Another example would be an all-ivory
combination: blazer, blouse, pants or skirt, and shoes.

Where to Wear This Look

Because this look is the most powerful of the seven
looks, someone who wears it has very high credibility, but will also appear intimidating and unapproachable. Some of the best places to wear the Sophisticate
Look are in cities, executive offices, political arenas,
financial institutions, religious positions, fund-raising
jobs, when giving public speeches or business pre-
sentations, and in highly competitive social situations,
especially with other women.

How Women Respond to This Look

Women automatically perceive the Sophisticate woman
to be a perfectionist with a completely enviable
lifestyle. Among women this look is respected and
admired, and its very classic visual effect gives you

strong credibility. Although it may intimidate some women, they will still find it a look they covet and wish to have themselves—someday.

How Men Respond to This Look

Men relate to this look with great respect, although most of them don't actually care for it visually. Men over fifty years of age enjoy having their wife or lady friend wear a Sophisticate Look because it proves they are successful and able to provide their woman with beautiful amenities. Men under fifty, however, often consider this look to be too unapproachable and sometimes classify it as a "rich bitch" look.

How Children Respond to This Look

The Sophisticate Look often makes children stand taller and sit up straight because of its authoritarian appearance. Children, like men, do not cuddle up to the Sophisticate woman. They generally become more polite and less comfortable in her presence.

The Gamin Look

Characteristic The use of all prints

Mood Youthful, friendly, energetic, spontaneous, approachable

How to Create This Look

A multicolored print dress is an example of the Gamin Look; or a separates look in which each piece is patterned, like the illustration shown here. Note the pin-dot blouse, plaid skirt, embroidered jacket, and patterned scarf—a typical Gamin Look during the Town and Country Cycle, which emphasizes separates so much.

Where to Wear This Look

Since the overwhelming perception of this look is of a person who is youthful, friendly, and approachable, someone wearing a Gamin Look would be considered cute and easy to get along with. Some of the best places to wear this look would be with young children, senior citizens, at social gatherings, graduations, weddings, in schools, service careers, one-to-one outings, courting, singles' bars, church gatherings, professions that deal with helping the public, in many sales situations, travelling, out to dinner with your husband or best beau, meeting people for the first time, and anywhere you want the other person to shine and feel welcome in your presence.

How Women Respond to This Look

Women will rarely compliment you when you wear this look, unless the print is very unusual. They will, however, respond to you in a congenial and confiding manner. This look will make you the easiest person to be around at any event.

How Men Respond to This Look

Not all men enjoy all prints, but most of them respond immediately to the youthful energy of colorful prints. In many cases, men will respond to you sexually because the Gamin Look seems feminine and very approachable. It puts men at ease and makes them feel comfortable and playful around you. If you are single, this look is vital to your wardrobe if you want to have men in your life, and if you are married, the Gamin Look will keep your husband happy. Even those women who like "classic," high-credibility looks should have at least one Gamin Look in their wardrobe at all times—life can become entirely too lonely and dull without it!

How Children Respond to This Look

In a Gamin Look, you become one of the gang. All the kids will love to be around you, but don't expect to command too much respect in this look. You will give them the feeling that you are full of youthful energy and they will want to be entertained and frolic with you.

The Romantic Look

Characteristic   The use of ruffly, illusionary, or
sheer fabrics

Mood   Feminine, delicate, naive, sweet,
enchanting

How to Create This Look

A sheer, ruffly white dress would be a Romantic
Look. The illustration shows eyelet pieces used as
separates to create a Romantic Look typical of the
Town and Country Cycle. Fabrics that are almost
always Romantic in effect include voile, eyelet, angora,
and lace.

Where to Wear This Look

This look creates a strongly feminine effect, and a
woman wearing a Romantic Look would be received
as ultra-female. The best places to wear this look
would be anniversary parties, birthday parties, or
weddings (as long as you choose a color that doesn't
overshadow the bride); out for an intimate breakfast,
lunch, or dinner with your favorite man; and on pic-
nics and Sunday afternoon outings, to singles' parties,
proms, ballroom or tea dances, and anytime you want
a man to respond to you in an old-fashioned, romantic way.

How Women Respond to This Look

When you wear a Romantic Look, you will rarely re-
ceive compliments from women who are your peers.
Older women may compliment you by mentioning

the beauty of the fabric rather than by commenting on how beautiful you yourself look. Women feel that this is a weak or uncomfortable look, but even when they don't relate to it personally, they may realize its power with men. If you wear too much of the Romantic Look around someone else's husband or boyfriend, you might get yourself into a bit of conflict.

How Men Respond to This Look

Pretty would be the word most frequently used by men when describing this look. Just as with the Gamin Look, the Romantic Look is most appealing to men. When you wear it, men will want to take care of you, protect you, sit quietly and admire you, or be alone with you. Of all the seven looks, it seems to be the most seductive to men. It is much less obvious than the Exotic Look (described later) because the Romantic Look conveys naiveté, and this subtlety is sexy. Romantic Look lingerie should be a must in your wardrobe, especially if you want to keep your man happy but can't quite force yourself to wear public Romantic Looks. Try it; your man's reaction will eventually convince you.

How Children Respond to This Look

Children love it; they will want to cuddle you and tell you they love you.

The Patrician Look

Characteristic The use of two equally balanced solid colors or prints

Mood Dignified, professional, prudent, serious, well-educated

How to Create This Look

One example of this look is a solid-color dress with contrasting collar and cuffs, as in this illustration. A separates Patrician Look would be, for example, a navy blazer and skirt with a white blouse and shoes. You can use prints, too: a red, white, and blue print dress with blue and white pin-dot cuffs has the balance that gives you a Patrician Look.

Where to Wear This Look

The Patrician Look has almost as much credibility as the Sophisticate Look, but is not as intimidating. Since it is so well balanced visually, it is a perfect look to wear when there is a job that needs to be done. The Patrician Look gives others the feeling that you are a loyal, hard-working person, but not too unapproachable. The best places to wear this look are in business or professional offices, political campaigns, legal offices, board meetings, investment clubs, business or professional organizations, and anywhere you need to assure those about you that you are a no-nonsense, dedicated, and loyal person to have around.

How Women Respond to This Look

Women will most often respond to this look with great respect. They will assume that you are a women who is definitely career-oriented. Because it is so similar to the Sophisticate Look, women generally assume that the Patrician woman has everything in her life under organized control.

How Men Respond to This Look

Research shows that men favor visual balance, so they are very comfortable with this look for professional and business women. In business this look will do a lot for a woman in a male environment—it has good credibility without being too intimidating. Socially, men will have a neutral response to it.

How Children Respond to This Look

Children respond with a great deal of respect. It would be good for maintaining authority without being too scary, but they'll never expect you to play with them as equals.

The Exotic Look

Characteristic   Uses evening fabrics such as velvet, satin, taffeta, and moiré, and/or garments cut to make a woman look sexy

Mood   Sexual, daring, worldly, dramatic, alluring

How to Create This Look

A halter-top evening gown like this one is an Exotic Look, as are tuxedos on women, strapless or one-shoulder gowns—all in evening fabrics.

Where to Wear This Look

Women who wear this look are often referred to as being gorgeous and sexy. Therefore, the best places to wear this look are any black-tie events, opera, theatre, ballet and symphony galas, casinos, parties during the Christmas season, and when entertaining in your home.

How Women Respond to This Look

Nearly everyone responds to this look with a "Wow!" —but from women this is often accompanied by a slight tone of envy. Most women are nervous about wearing the Exotic Look because it is both expensive and daring, and they convince themselves that it's not that important in their wardrobe. They admire it from a distance but may react with jealousy; they often wish they were young enough and thin enough to get away with it!

How Men Respond to This Look

The interesting thing about a man's reaction to this look is that although the Exotic Look can be quite sexy and appealing, it may also be somewhat un-approachable. This may partly be because most women who wear this look are being escorted by an-other man. Another problem with this look is that many women choose the color black—a color much more appealing to women than to men. While many men are very proud of having their woman in an Exotic Look, there are also men who don't like their wife or girlfriend wearing it because they feel uncom-fortable having everyone stare at her. Whatever reac-tion people have to this look, one thing is sure—the person wearing it will not go unnoticed.

How Children Respond to This Look

They are awed by your splendor and lonesome be-cause they know you are going out for the evening and they will be left out.

The Docent Look

Characteristic   Art-to-wear that presents a realistic image on a solid or print background

Mood   Arty, unique, imaginative, courageous, interesting

How to Create This Look

The large, realistic parrots on the skirt in this illustration make this separates treatment a Docent Look. Another example would be a white dress with a lion's head woven into a major portion of the dress. Jewelry can also have a Docent effect—for example, necklaces or belt buckles that are large animal heads.

Where to Wear This Look

Because this look has such an obvious image, it gives the woman wearing it, as well as the people meeting her, an instant conversation piece. This look can often be used as an icebreaker at difficult, crowded events where you don't know anybody. Some of the other situations where the Docent Look is appropriate are art openings, cultural events of all kinds, large cocktail parties, newcomer social events, large celebration parties, when you are meeting strangers, amusement parks ("My daughter is the one with the panda bears appliquéd on her sweater"), and when entertaining in your home.

How Women Respond to This Look

When women see this look in the store, their usual reaction is that they could only wear the outfit once, because everyone would recognize it the second time around. However, when they see it on someone else, they immediately begin talking about the design and feel comfortable with the wearer. Because of its drama and individuality, the Docent Look could easily make any woman the most memorable person in the room, as well as the easiest person to strike up a conversation with under difficult social conditions. If you are often in situations where you meet new people at crowded parties, you should certainly consider adding this look to your wardrobe.

How Men Respond to This Look

Men respond just as women do—it's easy and fun to start a conversation with someone wearing something this unusual.

How Children Respond to This Look

Children love to have a common something to talk about with adults. They can't figure out why you're wearing something so out of the ordinary, but they enjoy asking you questions about it.

Variations of the Seven Looks

Not everything in the world fits tidily into the categories I've defined as the Seven Looks, and personally, I wouldn't want them to. Looks, like people's moods, have subtle variations that add interest and useful adaptations to your wardrobe. In fact, I call them the Seven Variations.

Any look can be varied by adding an accent from another look.

Any look can be varied by adding an accent from another of the looks. For example, if you were going to be in a situation where you wanted to have high credibility with a man, but would like him to remember you are a woman too, try wearing a Sophisticate Look—all one color—but make one of the pieces a Romantic fabric like lace or eyelet. This would be Sophisticate Look, Romantic Variation.

There are exactly 49 ways to present yourself to the world.

Don't think you have to memorize all seven variations of each look. When you realize that there are exactly 49 ways to present yourself to the world, you may feel like you're about to take a final test in a hard subject. Relax! This approach simply helps you think about all the various ways you can use your clothes to give other people the impression you want them to have.

I've provided a chart of examples of the Seven Variations of the Seven Looks on pages 104 and 105—this is just to give you a feeling for how to adapt each look. Of course, a variation assigned to its own look—for example, Gamin Look/Gamin Variation—is simply the purest form of that look. If you understand the essentials of the looks, you'll have no trouble understanding how to use each one to vary each of the others. Try reading down the column under one of the looks, and you'll see what I mean.

Why are the variations important? Many of my clients can't afford to have every possible look in their wardrobe. Their lifestyle demands a lot of one or two looks, but they can get some of the effects of all seven looks by adding accents to their primary looks.

For example: If my client is the chief executive officer of a company and has a high-profile lifestyle, I would probably choose the Sophisticate Look as her major wardrobe mood. I would then accent her wardrobe with the seven variations of this look.

Sophisticate Look/Sophisticate Variation would give her the purest form—a powerful look suitable for running board meetings.

*Sophisticate Look/
Sophisticate Variation*

Sophisticate Look/Town and Country Variation would give her the ability to use her separates to create a sporty mood—a lower-key look that might be good for a company ballgame or for going to a League of Women Voters meeting.

*Sophisticate Look/
T&C Variation*

Sophisticate Look/Gamin Variation would add prints to her wardrobe—a useful look for when she wants to put someone at his ease rather than impress him.

*Sophisticate Look/
Gamin Variation*

Sophisticate Look/Patrician Variation allows her to use two different colors together, good for extending the usefulness of each piece, and giving her good credibility. This also is a useful travel technique—she can present the same pieces in a fresh way.

*Sophisticate Look/
Patrician Variation*

Sophisticate Look/Romantic Variation allows her to have feminine, sheer, or ruffly fabrics in her ward-

*Sophisticate Look/
Romantic Variation*

Variations of the Seven Looks

	TOWN AND COUNTRY LOOK *Tailored Separates*	SOPHISTICATE LOOK *All Solid*	GAMIN LOOK *All Prints*
Town and Country Variation	Navy blazer White blouse Gray skirt Navy shoes Print scarf	Black blazer Black dress Black stockings Black shoes Gold belt	Polka-dot blouse Plaid skirt
Sophisticate Variation	Navy blazer Navy tone-on-tone blouse Navy skirt Navy shoes Navy pin dot scarf	Black dress Black shoes Black belt Gold necklace	Tone-on-tone blouse in one color Tone-on-tone skirt in same color
Gamin Variation	Tweed blazer Polka-dot blouse Black onyx and Two-tone shoes	Black tone-on-tone dress Tweed skirt pearl necklace	Print blouse with matching print skirt
Romantic Variation	White eyelet blouse Navy pants Navy shoes	Black dress Inset black lace collar Black shoes	Sheer print ruffly dress Sandals
Patrician Variation	Navy blazer Gray blouse Navy skirt Gray shoes	Black dress Gold belt Gold necklace Black shoes	Two-tone print as in navy and yellow stripe Two-tone belt
Exotic Variation	White satin blouse Navy satin skirt Red belt Navy shoes	Black velvet dress Gold necklace Black stockings Black shoes	Print dress with bare shoulders or back
Docent Variation	White sweater with appliqued butterfly Navy pants Navy shoes	Black dress Large brass tiger-head belt Black shoes	Dress with background print and one foreground design

ROMANTIC LOOK	PATRICIAN LOOK	EXOTIC LOOK	DOCENT LOOK
Ruffly, Sheer	*Two Balanced Colors*	*Bare, Sexy, After Five*	*Art To Wear*
Ruffly print blouse Solid skirt Wide belt	White sweater Navy scarf Navy skirt Navy/white shoes	One piece dress with blouse, belt and skirt in different colors Solid shoes	Panda bears on red sweater Black solid skirt Black boots/shoes
Sheer dress with with see-through lace overlaid (both in same color)	White dress Gold piping on collar and cuffs White shoes	Black velvet dress Rhinestone necklace Black shoes	Green solid dress with pearl flower design in one place
Ruffly dress in soft delicate print Sandals	Print dress in stripe Polka dot collar and cuffs	Multi-color sequin dress Bare shoulders Sandals	Polka dot dress with one large design in several colors
Sheer, ruffly solid-color dress with lace trim	Sheer solid dress with lace collar and cuffs	Very sheer lacy dress Sandals	Lacy dress with one woven flower design
White eyelet blouse Red skirt White eyelet slip—showing Red sandals	Solid dress Collar and cuffs of another color Two-tone shoe	Satin solid color dress Gold piping Gold belt Gold shoes	Solid color dress White piping One white design
Sheer, lacy off-the-shoulder solid dress Matching sandals	Black velvet dress with gold piping at neck and waist	Bare gold lamé dress (floor length) Gold shoes	Long white caftan with lion's head imprinted on fabric
Embroidered flowers appliquéd on sheer dress	Solid dress design on blouse and on skirt balanced	Black velvet dress with rhinestone flower design	Dress with very little background color All design

robe, and to achieve the apparently conflicting goals of appearing both powerful and feminine.

Sophisticate Look/
Exotic Variation

Sophisticate Look/Exotic Variation allows her to use evening fabrics and achieve a sexier mood.

Sophisticate Look/
Docent Variation

Sophisticate Look/Docent Variation is a way to incorporate interesting art-to-wear that she may pick up on business trips. It allows her to meet people easily when she is at crowded events and "off-duty."

Chapter 6 will explore the use of the Seven Looks and their variations in specific career and social situations.

What Looks Do You Wear Now?

Most people naturally favor one particular look—maybe they have unconsciously noticed that other people responded well to them in that look, or perhaps it is the look they were trained to wear by their parents and social group. Or they may even be unconscious that they're sticking so closely to a single look, and that this is affecting the way other people react to them.

When I work with a new client, I don't try to completely change the looks she has in her wardrobe—I just want her to be aware of what her wardrobe choices are saying about her and to get her to try to expand a little into looks and variations that might fulfill other needs.

This is a good time to take a look at *your* wardrobe—what is it saying about you? What facets of yourself can you bring out by adding new looks, or by accenting your major look with variations from other looks?

Checklist Exercise

Check all the things that appeal to you in the following seven groups. Don't try to be practical, or to guess which things you *should* like; just check everything you now wear and would like to wear, or things that you like to look at, or feel, or even think about. You can check as many things in each group as you wish.

Group 1
- ☐ charm bracelets
- ☐ low-heeled shoes
- ☐ practical fabrics
- ☐ easy-to-wear garments
- ☐ textured fabrics
- ☐ corduroy
- ☐ flannel
- ☐ wash-and-wear fabrics
- ☐ sweaters
- ☐ blazers
- ☐ digital watch
- ☐ narrow belts
- ☐ casual clothes
- ☐ tailored clothes
- ☐ bulky knits
- ☐ tweeds
- ☐ socks
- ☐ cotton underwear
- ☐ chain necklaces
- ☐ scarves
- ☐ natural fibers
- ☐ plaid wools

Group 2
- ☐ best quality
- ☐ classic clothes
- ☐ severe lines
- ☐ dominant colors
- ☐ elegant fabrics
- ☐ gold buttons
- ☐ linen
- ☐ wool
- ☐ cashmere
- ☐ gabardine
- ☐ gold jewelry
- ☐ unusual accessories
- ☐ leather gloves
- ☐ gold/diamond watch
- ☐ matching shoes & handbag
- ☐ neutral colors
- ☐ fur coat
- ☐ costume jewelry
- ☐ large earrings
- ☐ pumps
- ☐ dresses
- ☐ matching garments
- ☐ belts
- ☐ large shawls
- ☐ fur trim
- ☐ suede
- ☐ leather
- ☐ simplicity

107

Group 3
- [ ] stripes
- [ ] gay, unusual details
- [ ] latest fads
- [ ] special trimming
- [ ] patchwork
- [ ] plastic jewelry
- [ ] garnets
- [ ] calico prints
- [ ] rickrack trim
- [ ] plaids
- [ ] Mickey Mouse watch
- [ ] jade
- [ ] pleats
- [ ] being different
- [ ] offbeat fabrics
- [ ] bright colors
- [ ] cute prints
- [ ] polka dots
- [ ] taffeta
- [ ] pearls
- [ ] mixed-fabric shoes
- [ ] colorful accessories
- [ ] dramatic fabric combinations
- [ ] whimsical buttons
- [ ] two-tone shoes
- [ ] several colors at the same time

Group 4
- [ ] color contrast
- [ ] two solid colors
- [ ] balance
- [ ] piping trims
- [ ] tank watch
- [ ] spectator shoes
- [ ] matching belt & shoes
- [ ] solid-color scarves
- [ ] two-tone stripes
- [ ] reversible raincoat
- [ ] suits
- [ ] white collars & cuffs
- [ ] body stockings
- [ ] contrasting overstitching
- [ ] colored hose
- [ ] few accessories
- [ ] business looks
- [ ] plain handbags
- [ ] blended colors
- [ ] wearing basic colors

Group 5
- [ ] being pretty
- [ ] ruffles
- [ ] flowing fabrics
- [ ] soft lines
- [ ] pastel colors
- [ ] gathering
- [ ] chiffon
- [ ] voile & sheer fabrics
- [ ] lace
- [ ] pure silk
- [ ] floral chintzes
- [ ] angora

☐ shirring   ☐ wrinkled linen & cotton
☐ braiding   ☐ delicate jewelry

Group 6
☐ low-cut dresses   ☐ dramatic entrances
☐ voluptuous necklines   ☐ feathers
☐ cut-out bodices   ☐ sequins
☐ velvet   ☐ brocade fabrics
☐ glittery things   ☐ faille fabrics
☐ gold lame   ☐ tight sweaters
☐ colored furs   ☐ high heels
☐ rhinestones   ☐ strappy sandals
☐ garter belts   ☐ metallic shoes
☐ sexy underwear   ☐ diamond watch
☐ satin   ☐ dramatic costume jewelry

Group 7
☐ dramatic figures   ☐ metal figures as jewelry
☐ art-to-wear   ☐ poodle skirts
☐ embroidery   ☐ animal-head belt buckles
☐ a single large design   ☐ appliques
☐ small hand details   ☐ woven designs
☐ sculptured fabrics   ☐ tapestry
☐ batik   ☐ painted shoes
☐ tie-dyed fabrics   ☐ needlepoint handbags
☐ hand-painted silk   ☐ whimsical T-shirts

To find out where your instinctive fashion personality falls, count the check marks you made in each group and tally them below. After you count your check marks, go back and put dots next to the items that you actually *have* in your wardrobe now or *have had* in the past.

	Check Marks	*Dots*
Group 1	_____	_____
Group 2	_____	_____
Group 3	_____	_____
Group 4	_____	_____
Group 5	_____	_____
Group 6	_____	_____
Group 7	_____	_____

Ideally, you will have some check marks in each group. If you find that in some groups you have far more check marks than dots, that's a look that you should consider adding more of in your wardrobe—you may not be expressing these moods in your current wardrobe choices. If you find this pattern in most of the seven groups, you are probably not enjoying what you wear as much as you should.

If the number of check marks and dots are about equal in most of the groups, you are probably choosing appropriate clothing for your lifestyle as well as for your mood changes. You are probably enjoying what you wear.

If almost all of your check marks and dots fall into one or two groups, you should try experimenting with another look that could give other people a whole new view of you and expand your feelings about your personal possibilities. Chapter 6 will give you some ideas about this.

Here are the groups and their corresponding looks:

Group 1   Town and Country Look
Group 2   Sophisticate Look
Group 3   Gamin Look
Group 4   Patrician Look
Group 5   Romantic Look
Group 6   Exotic Look
Group 7   Docent Look

The Seven Looks and their Seven Variations give you a wonderful way to get the most out of your clothes—you can get a good return on your clothing investment because you can vary the way you look, and you can also create the image you want. You can give yourself credibility and even power when you need it, and you can make other people feel relaxed around you when you want to see some friendly faces or need to help them.

Color has a potent effect on people, too. Chapter 5 will give you a lot of new ideas about how you can use color to increase the impact of the looks you choose.

5.   Color Impact

Have you had your colors analyzed? Even if you haven't, you are probably aware that there has been a color revolution in fashion, with any number of color theories available to help you discover which colors are most flattering to you.

You may even have done your own color analysis by reading Carol Jackson's best-selling book *Color Me Beautiful*. Her theory established the "seasonal" approach to color analysis. Like most of the theories, it is based on the idea that everyone's skin and hair coloring has either warm or cool undertones, and that you should learn to recognize the colors that have warm or cool undertones in order to choose clothes and jewelry that blend with your skin and hair tones.

In the seasonal theory, warm tones are further divided into the pale range (Spring) and intense range (Autumn), while the cool tones are divided into pale tones (Summer) and intense tones (Winter). Your coloring determines which season's colors you should wear. For example, a brunette with very fair skin and hazel eyes would probably be a Winter; if you have red highlights in your hair and dark golden brown eyes, you would be considered an Autumn. A Summer might be someone with rosy pink skin, blue eyes, and ash blonde hair; and someone with vivid red hair, ivory skin, and pale blue eyes would be a Spring.

Many color theories are available to help you discover which colors are most flattering to you.

113

Another color theory that I find useful comes originally from the Ameritone paint company, and divides colors into Color Key 1, the pink undertones, and Color Key 2, the yellow undertones. This means that no matter what your coloring, if you want to wear black or navy or red, you may, as long as you choose a tone that is on your color key. I like this theory better than the seasonal one because it expands your horizon of color choices considerably.

Color theory has added a lot to the effectiveness people have in creating an attractive wardrobe for themselves. Many women—and men too—have been able to reduce the number of color mistakes they make when they buy clothing, and their attention to color tones has been improved. They can be sure, if they stick to their color season or color key, that their clothes' colors will be flattering.

I have found that most of the women I have worked with are already attracted to their best colors, although they have often settled on a very narrow range of tones because they feel pretty and safe in those colors. Color analysis often helps them understand why those colors are good on them, and encourages them to try out a wider range than they originally thought were good on them.

But there are problems with staying strictly within a defined color group.

I encourage you to learn all you can about color theory, and especially to develop your eye for the subtle differences of tone that tell you whether you are looking at a color with a blue/pink undertone or a yellow undertone. But there are problems with staying strictly within a defined color group.

For example, as I explained in the last chapter about the Seven Looks, there are certain looks that contribute credibility and power that you may need

114

on some occasions to achieve your personal goals. Color also has strong subconscious meaning, and in certain situations, you cannot be limited to your best colors. If you work in the financial community, you *must* include black and navy blue in your wardrobe, whether or not they appear in your color analyst's list of good colors for you.

Color has a strong subconscious meaning, and in certain situations, you cannot be limited to your best colors.

Another problem is that certain colors and tones dominate during each of the three fashion cycles (discussed in Chapter 3). The Sophisticate Cycle is particularly notable, with its black, ivory, and very intense jewel colors. Many women who stay strictly within their color group have trouble finding colors in their range during the whole five years of a cycle. This can lead them into buying fabric and sewing their own clothes; but even if they are expert seamstresses, they're unable to find accessories to complement their homesewn garments and can end up with an outdated look.

You will also miss a lot of fashion fun if you refuse to play with the color groups that fabric manufacturers introduce each season. You will find that a certain range of colors shows up each year, blended in prints and plaids, and in complementary solid separates. In some years you won't be able to find much that works on your seasonal palette. *But you don't have to be a slave to your color palette!*

You will miss a lot of fashion fun if you refuse to play with each season's color groups.

I'm going to teach you how to take advantage of colors that would work well in your lifestyle and wardrobe, but that are not a natural blend with your skintones and hair color. But first, let's consider what psychological effects colors have on other people so that you can think about which ones might be useful to you in your lifestyle.

115

How People Respond to Colors

Just as music creates moods and feelings, so does color—it can express the subtlest emotions, especially when thoughtfully used in combination with the Seven Looks and their variations. Color is also the most immediate and overwhelming message received by other people about what you're wearing; they'll be aware of your dress's color before they notice its cut or quality, and before they notice the color of your eyes. This response is often completely unconscious, and all the more powerful because of that.

Color is the most immediate and over-whelming message received by other people about what you're wearing.

I have provided a chart of colors and their most common associations. Take a few minutes and scan it to get a feeling for the unconscious reactions each color tends to get. Note that I've arranged the colors in order of their power: in other words, if you want high credibility in what you're wearing on a particular day, you should wear one of the first six colors on the chart; but if you want to have a friendly day during which people will be comfortable around you, choose one of the other colors or combine one of the less powerful colors with the powerful one to make yourself more approachable.

Observe people in the next few days, and notice your own natural reactions when you first meet someone. You'll probably first notice the color of their whole garment, then you'll notice how it's put together (which you could identify as Town and Country Look, or Gamin Look and so on), and finally, you'll notice the overall shape, which is really the cycle's line. These impressions will give you an idea

The Psychological Attributes of Colors
(Arranged from High to Low Credibility)

Color	*Most Common Reaction*
Black	Credible, reliable, confident, honest, intelligent, discriminating, perfectionist, intimidating, powerful, self-sufficient, independent, opinionated, reserved, decisive, prosperous
Navy	Trustworthy, practical, productive, wise, conservative, poised, educated, logical, professional, expert, wealthy, reserved, dependable, loyal, influential, decisive
Brown	Organized, conformist, thrifty, enduring, determined, physical, secure, eloquent, sensitive, protective, social, virile, content, comfortable, idealistic, cautious, affectionate, peaceful, earthy
Gray	Supportive, private, inquisitive, experienced, statistical, stable, team-oriented, objective, decisive, just, detailed, sympathetic, industrious, persistent, defensive, skillful, economical
Ivory	Pure, content, elegant, particular, formal, mannered, graceful, tolerant, patient, calm, enduring, honorable, dignified, respectful, serene, polished

Red Ambitious, exciting, risky, expressive, impulsive, eccentric, active, humorous, dominant, competitive, original, alluring, bold, dramatic, imaginative, leader, sexual, unique, intense, risk-taker, impetuous

White Virginal, unspoiled, virtuous, giving, respectful, enchanting, free, precious, healthy, cheerful, unbiased, kind, tender, youthful, spirited, affectionate, sweet, supportive, dependent

Yellow Daring, argumentative, clever, charming, spontaneous, outdoorsy, captivating, inquisitive, proud, enlightened, steadfast, gregarious, jovial, envious, worldly, saucy

Green Languid, defensive, passive, materialistic, determined, inadequate, abrupt, ardent, idealistic, affable, moderate, optimistic, critical, stubborn, calculating, analytical, long-suffering, fickle, neighborly

Beige Intelligent, utilitarian, shy, vague, liberal, prudent, indifferent, consistent, painstaking, possessive, self-sacrificing, absolute, superior, hospitable, independent, sympathetic, methodical, modest, conforming, serious, reserved, learned, orderly, deductive, frugal, well-bred, volunteer

Pink, Peach	Charming, tender, passive, demure, delicate, impetuous, coquetish, naive, loving, beloved, romantic, blissful, generous, spirited, capricious, enthusiastic, simple, congenial, lithe, cooperative, sweet, inexperienced
Orange	Obstinate, pert, whimsical, frivolous, winsome, animated, naughty, rainbow-chaser, immature, friendly, impertinent, inventive, arbitrary, comical, permissable, rebellious, opportunist, emphathetic, curious, enjoyable, impulsive, pretentious, energetic

Note: Shadings of the above colors, such as blue for the color navy, share the same attributes as the stronger colors from which they originate.

of what kind of person they are, how much money they have, and what kind of life they lead. Whether or not your impression is correct, they will have trouble countering it by what they say or do.

Another interesting thing to observe is that people tend to compliment others when they're wearing their own best colors. For example, in seasonal terms, my husband was a definite Spring, while I am a Winter; he most often complimented me when I was wearing *his* colors—peach, coral, turquoise, aqua, and shades of violet, even though these are not my best colors.

Men and women often respond very differently to colors. This is useful information to have, because it means that the colors *you* especially love may not be working for you when you are with men, even though the women you see give you enthusiastic compliments. Or if you are going to be primarily with women, you'll do well to wear the colors *they* respond well to.

The colors you expecially love may not be working for you when you're with men.

119

How Men and Women Respond to Colors

Women like muted tones, neutral colors like oatmeal, beige, and burlap, and they like black. Most women would characterize these colors as sophisticated and elegant. Women respond well to olive green and acid green, and they like combinations of these muted and neutral tones. Women also respond very well to black and the other power colors. Any of these colors are excellent choices if you are planning what to wear to a women's club meeting or any other situation when you will be relating to other women.

The colors I've just listed as those that women like best are just the colors that men like least. They do not respond well to muted shades like grayed pastels and mauves; they actively dislike olive green, or almost any shade of green other than kelly green; they don't like gray on women, and the paler the gray, the less they like it; and sophisticated neutrals like oatmeal and beige leave them cold.

What men like best are clear, bright tones, and they almost always love prints in bright colors. They respond romantically to pink, peach, and red.

What men like best are clear, bright tones, and they almost always love prints in bright colors. They respond romantically to pink, peach, and red, probably because they're fleshtones. Reds are a little tricky, because they tend not to like orange-reds, preferring true reds and burgundy colors as long as they're not too muted. They seem to like blue, especially cobalt blue; although navy is a business color and they'll only respond to it in a businesslike way.

The odd thing about black, which has always had a sexual image, is that men do not respond romantically to it at all, probably because it's too dominant a color. They may feel proud to have a woman in a

120

beautiful black evening dress on their arm, but they'll be unlikely to hold your hand or murmur sweet nothings in your ear, no matter how flattering black may be on you.

Men seem to like color contrasts, while women like blends of close colors. For example, women love ivory and camel together, and men don't; but put camel with black for contrast, and men respond well. I think that it's possible that men and women actually *see* colors differently—that men can't make the fine distinctions in tone that women can, and so prefer strong colors and strong color contrasts.

Men and women respond alike to the dark power colors—black, navy, brown, and gray—in business situations. You will seem strong and credible to either sex, but neither men nor women will feel cozy around you in them. Ivory is sometimes a good choice, because it has good credibility but seems warm to women and feminine to men; to some extent it allows you to accomplish conflicting goals.

You will seem strong and credible to either sex in the dark power colors.

Breaking Your Color Rules

Some people's color analysts have given them a color palette that is too weak for their lifestyle. If they try to perform in a leadership role while always wearing soft pastel colors, they'll never get the respect they need, whether or not these colors blend well with their own coloring.

On the other hand, Winters like myself have the opposite problem; I have black hair, ivory skin, and hazel eyes. Some of my best natural colors are black, true red, pure white, gray, hot pink, royal purple, true blue, emerald green, and lemon yellow, with silver-toned accessories rather than yellow gold. When I wear these colors, I feel attractive and tend to get compliments, so naturally I gravitate to them when I decorate my home or office, or buy a new car.

However, all Winters tend to look dominant and slightly intimidating, especially in those strong colors. As I did the research that led to my wardrobe theories, I decided to try using my Winter colors for business and social situations in which I needed control and credibility—lecturing, for example—and found that these colors worked beautifully for me in those circumstances. On the other hand, when I wanted to have fun and be one of the gang, I started wearing colors that fall more into the Spring and Autumn categories. The response was terrific, because people are generally more comfortable with warm colors.

I found that even in patterned fabrics (for a Gamin Look) I could retain high credibility in, say, a black and white print; but that in a mahogany, camel, and gold tweed blazer I became everyone's friend and confidante but no longer looked like a professional woman, or high-profiled socialite.

A knowledge of color and of the Seven Looks and their variations gives you a very powerful personal tool.

I have come to realize that when you combine a knowledge of the psychological effects of color and the Seven Looks and their variations, you have a very powerful tool for achieving your day-to-day personal goals.

You need to know everything you can about color theories and what colors are best for you. But if your lifestyle needs a broader range of colors, don't limit yourself to your best colors. Learn those theories, and then learn how to break the rules.

There are two effective ways to wear a color that isn't in your color palette: By combining the color with one that *is* in your range; and by effective use of makeup.

It's easy to learn to combine colors. If you look wonderful in black, put it with the camel or beige that you theoretically can't wear; the contrast is wonderful. Or if you *can't* wear black but need a black suit for your job as a stockbroker—go ahead, buy the suit. Then wear a blouse that is in a color you *can* wear— ivory might be an excellent choice, or an ivory and black print. The blouse's collar will be near your face and will counteract the draining effect of the black suit jacket.

Even if black is a great color for you, remember that powerful colors like black need strong makeup to provide visual balance. If black is not a good color for you, your makeup needs to be not only strong, but corrective as well.

Powerful colors need strong makeup to provide visual balance.

Makeup Techniques to Support Your Color Choices

When you wear your best natural colors, your makeup routine can be quite simple—a natural foundation, lipstick, blush, and mascara will make you look fresh. Just intensify the effect if you are wearing strong colors.

But supposing you need to wear a color that isn't in your color range. With fairly uncomplicated makeup techniques, I have given women all over the country the possibility of wearing any color they wish. All you need to know is where your own coloring fits on the seasonal chart or on the Color Key concept—do you look best in colors with warm, yellow undertones, or with cool, pink undertones?

Black is a Winter's color. If I am working with a woman who does not have Winter coloring but needs to wear black in her work, I simply redesign her makeup to make her look more like a Winter.

Redesign your makeup to look like the season of the garment you'll wear.

The first change I make is her foundation. I look at the black garment she wants to wear and determine whether it has a yellow undertone or a pink undertone. If yellow, I choose a light shade of beige foundation, and if pink, I use a light bisque or ivory porcelain shade. When I am uncertain of the undertone, I choose a shade one degree lighter than the one she is currently wearing.

Eye makeup is important, because the eyes are the most useful feature in distracting attention from the color black. No matter what their eyelash or brow color, I have my clients use black mascara, black eyebrow coloring, black liner, and a soft black or charcoal pencil stroked across the crease of the eye just above the eyelid.

Eye shape determines the emphasis for eyeliner, but I have clients use the liner primarily inside the eyelash line, just above the lower lashes and just under the upper lashes, keeping the strongest concentration of color at the outside corner of the eye. I have most women leave their eyelids free of makeup so that their eyes have depth; their eyes usually look best if they appear to recede into the shadow created in the lids' crease.

ery sophisticated eye,
or black. It works for
h clothes in brown,
a matching shade as

ends on my client's
who has difficulty
and blusher that are
he is a Summer, I
nd blusher. If she is
blue-red.
, you must *exactly*
your clothes if you
r colors containing
magenta, fuschia,
don't match these
ed by the color of
ar is complemen-

aking color rules
is not naturally
makeup. If you
that you can get
agined!

If you are wearing a color that is not naturally flattering, use that color in your makeup.

Looks can be adapted by accents
from one of the Seven Variations, so can your best
colors be mixed with accents from one of the other
three groups. Use the patterned fabrics in your ward-

125

robe to lead you into other pieces in a color you don't usually wear, or add scarves or jewelry to pick up colors you have thought of as taboo for you.

Or go all the way, and buy all the pieces in a color you want to add, and adjust your makeup accordingly. The world of color is open to you.

6.   Clothes That
        Get Results

How do you choose what you're going to wear each morning? If you're like most people, you probably make intuitive decisions: You feel a bit low, and you think perhaps your red silk shirt will cheer you up, or your black suit always makes you feel like a successful executive, and you're going to talk to someone you need to impress.

The color, texture, and pattern of your clothes have a direct effect on how people respond to you. This chapter is going to relate all these effects to the different needs you have in your lifestyle. If you master this material you can pull those intuitive decisions into consciousness and be one of the very few people who make their clothes do the right psychological job for them in their business and personal lives.

The color, texture, and pattern of your clothes have a direct effect on how people respond to you.

A great deal of this chapter will talk about how to dress for specific careers, because effective career clothes should be very conservative for some jobs, and very creative, even wild, for other jobs. Many of my clients and readers are women who have made homemaking their career, and I will deal also with effective ways to dress for homemaking roles as well as for leadership roles in women's clubs.

The same principles, by the way, are generally true for both men and women, although the applications often differ. I'm going to include examples of how these principles affect men at work. And don't forget what you learned in the last chapter—men and women perceive color differently, and you should include this knowledge in your choice of what to wear according to your audience.

I have noticed that women have a simple response to clothes: they see them as either powerful or not powerful. Men seem to have more complex reactions and are more susceptible to the psychology of clothes. If you are dealing primarily with men, you need to take into consideration that your own reactions to clothes are very different from theirs. Throughout the chapter, I'll mention how men and women react to specific looks.

Men seem to have more complex reactions and are more susceptible to the psychology of clothes.

A Quick Review of the Seven Looks

There are two things about your clothes that affect how people *unconsciously* perceive you: color, and which of the seven looks your clothes reflect. You just learned about the effects of color in the last chapter, but here's a quick review of the seven looks—I'm going to be referring to them a lot in this chapter.

The Town and Country Look

The Town and Country Look is basically the use of separates, and it ranges from a conservative dark suit with a blouse in a different color, to a Gamin variation that combines patterns in pleasing informality. Because it is often informal, it can be almost as friendly as Gamin.

In its more conservative variations, it's an essential look for jobs or situations that require other people to feel that you are stable and reliable.

Women respond very well to the Town and Country Look both on men and on other women, but don't expect to attract men romantically in this look—it's too close to the way men dress themselves.

The Sophisticate Look

This is the look of an outfit that is all one color. If it's a suit, the blouse, belt, and shoes are also the same solid color as the suit. A Sophisticate dress look has the belt and shoes in the same solid color as the dress.

This is the most powerful of the looks. It has very high credibility, but it is also intimidating, especially in power colors like black, navy, ivory, and red. You should be very selective about wearing this look around the office, and if you find yourself in conflict with other people at work, change over to other looks that are less intimidating and see if the conflict cools off.

Women will often compliment you on your Sophisticate outfit—women love it, even while seeing you as somewhat unapproachable. Men will see you as all business, and if they are not dressed as powerfully themselves, they may feel outpowered by you; this can be useful in a situation where you need the upper hand, or it can be counterproductive if you need an open, friendly relationship as equals.

It's the best possible look, however, if you have to make an important speech or presentation for which you need high credibility, or if you are in a negotiation for which you need a powerful image.

The Gamin Look

The Gamin Look is based on patterned fabrics. A print dress is Gamin; add a print blouse to a Town and Country Look, and you've got a Gamin variation. It's the friendliest, happiest look, and many ambitious women neglect this look at some cost to their careers.

People respond to prints with friendliness; it's precisely because prints have no power that they are so effective in making friends and helping people feel at ease with you. When you are wearing a Sophisticate Look, people will be impressed by you and want to represent themselves in the most impressive way they can. When you are wearing a Gamin Look, people may tell you secrets, and they will represent themselves more honestly, defects and all.

When I have a client coming to my office, I usually wear a Gamin Look because I want him or her to relax and pour out all their wardrobe frustrations and needs as openly as possible. If I wore a Sophisticate outfit, they would sit up straight and represent themselves as fully in charge of their clothing situation, because they would be coping with feeling less powerful than me.

Gamin fabrics include not only stripes and plaids, but also the very textured fabrics like raw silk; the texture becomes a subtle pattern in its warming effect on other people. Men can wear Gamin suits in light striped fabrics or striped seersucker.

Many male executives who always dress severely at the office have found that wearing a seersucker suit to a company social occasion outside the office has a surprising effect on their employees: People that don't usually approach them come around and talk, and informally tell them important things that they never would have been able to find out back at the office.

An interesting thing about Gamin looks is that women don't particularly *like* these clothes in their conscious mind. If you wear a nice patterned dress and actually ask someone if they like it, they will probably not rave about it. But they will nevertheless be very warm toward you without knowing that it's related to your print dress.

I'm going to be referring to the Gamin Look a lot in this chapter because it can get you amazing interpersonal results in the right context.

The Romantic Look

I'm sure you recognize a Romantic Look when you see one—it's ruffles and lace and eyelet, see-through tucked handkerchief linen, garden hats with streaming ribbons—clothes that are unmistakably feminine.

Obviously, the Romantic Look has an important place in your personal life. Men love you in it, and you feel feminine and lovely. But it can also have uses in the office as a variation on the sterner, businesslike looks.

For example, a woman lawyer whose male client looks baffled by the legal advice she's giving should try wearing a ruffled solid blouse under her conservative suit. She can't go so far as a patterned blouse at the office, because it would undermine her credibility, but the feminine ruffle might add a note of vulnerability that will make her client feel less intimidated and more able to understand what she's saying.

It's also very appropriate to wear a Romantic Look to a social business function that involves couples; it's probably better to wear this if you are with a man rather than alone, because other women will interpret this look as potentially predatory if you have no man of your own to impress with it.

The Patrician Look

A Patrician Look is one that combines two solid colors, usually with two items in each color: a solid dress with matching shoes and contrasting jacket and belt, or matching blouse and shoes with contrasting, matched skirt and jacket. This is the second most powerful look, especially in power colors, and the same cautions and uses apply as for Sophisticate looks.

The Exotic Look

The Exotic Look is basically evening dress at its most glamorous—black capes lined with scarlet for men; daringly bared evening dresses for women. The only careers this is appropriate for are those in the entertainment business—opera divas, nightclub singers, and theatre people, for example.

In your personal and social life it's a wonderful look. This is for the occasion when your man wants to show you off—"Look at the gorgeous, sexy woman I've got." Oddly enough, this look will make your man proud, but not particularly affectionate. He will be possessive, but won't make a single romantic move while he shows you off in your stunning black backless dress.

The Docent Look

The Docent Look is that of clothes-as-art. Examples are a sweater with a life-sized tiger woven into the wool, or a jumper that has a sunflower whose stem begins at the hem, and whose flower is bigger-than-life on the bodice.

Many versions of the Docent Look are too informal or outrageous for business offices. But not necessarily; I have a sweater with two panda bears on it that I combine with a black and white plaid skirt for a Town and Country Look that would work in less formal offices.

In sophisticated versions, the Docent Look is wonderful for people in the arts—a way to express individuality and creativity in their clothes. It's also good when you must go to large parties where you'll meet many strangers—it gives people a topic on which to approach you.

Now that we've reviewed the definitions and effects of the seven looks, let's begin by taking a look at the basics of dressing for business.

Some Basic Rules for Business Dressing

You're dressing for two audiences at work: your colleagues and your clients or customers. Your colleagues probably dress a lot like people do in all the other companies in your industry, with some subtle differences based on your company's own corporate culture and whether or not your company is located in a big city. Look around you at work and study how the men and women are dressed at different levels of responsibility.

If you are ambitious, dress exactly like your colleagues but go one grade higher in fabric quality.

If you are ambitious, the rule of thumb is: Dress exactly like your colleagues at the same level, but go one grade higher in fabric quality. This is true for both men and women, and for women's clubs as well as business. This approach works because you need the support of your colleagues in order to become a leader, and if you outdress them too much you will alienate them, but you also need to distinguish yourself as someone who cares about their image more than the average person does.

For example, if you are a corporate secretary who would like to become a marketing trainee, and all the secretaries wear mix-and-match Town and Country looks at the Evan Picone level, then you should choose mix-and-match clothes too, but invest in one or two blazers that are more expensive and have a more sophisticated cut than Evan Picone jackets. You shouldn't suddenly start wearing Sophisticate outfits that will outpower the other secretaries and leave you lunching alone all the time.

An equivalent male example would be an engineer with his eye on a management spot; he observes that his colleagues wear polyester pants and short-sleeved sports shirts with no tie. If he wants to get ahead, he should buy some well-cut pants in, say, gabardine, and some better-quality shirts that are still short-sleeved and informal. He might have a tie around for those occasions when top management does a site visit, but he shouldn't suddenly start wearing dark three-piece suits to work.

If, on the other hand, you love what you're doing and just want to be happy with your colleagues and don't even *want* a promotion, then you should dress just like they do and make sure you have lots of Gamin prints in your wardrobe—prints make everyone respond to you in a friendly way, and this will make you feel happy.

*If you just want
to be happy at
work, dress
exactly like your
colleagues and
include lots
of prints.*

Dressing for customers or clients is a more subtle undertaking, because you need to think about just exactly what you want to achieve *that day.* Here's a sales example: You're going to try to sell your company's services to a potential client that you know has a contract with a competitor. You have to woo the customer away and persuade him or her that your company has many benefits over their current supplier.

For the first sales call, you should wear a Gamin look, cleverly scaled to the expensiveness of the product you're selling. The more high-priced your service, the more expensive your Gamin look should be. The patterned fabric will make the person you're calling on feel friendly and confiding, and he's more likely to tell you the truth about the problems they're having with the other supplier, the political situation in his office that will affect the supplier decision, and just exactly what he's looking for in a new supplier.

Armed with this knowledge and ready with specific proposals on the second call, you should wear a look calculated to give you and your proposal a lot of credibility—a Patrician or Sophisticate look in a pretty color would be good.

Is the deal still not closed? And did the client waffle, unsure whether you could really deliver the services you're promising? On your next call, wear a Sophisticate Look in a power color—black, navy, red, or ivory. Your credibility will be very high, and a touch of intimidation may be just the thing to get him to sign the contract.

The level of dress in big cities is a lot more sophisticated than in smaller cities and suburbs.

Don't forget the effect of geography—the level of dress in companies in big cities is a lot more sophisticated than that in smaller cities and the suburbs. One young man adopted the executive look of his San Francisco high-flying high-tech company: expensive dark three-piece suits, silky shirts, and silk ties. When he interviewed for a higher-level job in a San Jose company, he wore his usual look and quickly recognized his error. "They thought I looked like a gigolo!" For his follow-up interview, he wore a conservative oxford cloth shirt and a quiet tie. He got the job.

Details matter. I see too many wonderful looks undermined by details like badly tended hair or shoes worn beyond salvation. If your career requires an expensive, conservative look, you cannot wear your dark suit with comfortable walking shoes with ripple soles, and expect your look to succeed. You need to wear well-polished, expensive-looking shoes, and the heels shouldn't be worn down.

When you consider what looks you are wearing to work, you may find that you've been creating effects that you don't like, but you can turn them around in no time.

One of my clients had an important job on the staff of a political figure. When she started, she had almost no money, but she bought one good-quality plaid wool skirt and several solid shirts to wear with it. This version of a Gamin Look had to be her entire wardrobe at the beginning of her career. Remembering it later, she told me that everyone was very friendly to her during that period and was always offering to help her or take her to dinner.

Then she married a very rich man and set up housekeeping in a wonderful penthouse. She continued in her job, where she was becoming very valuable to her politician-boss, but now she had all the money she could possibly want for her wardrobe. She went wild and bought lots of clothes, all Sophisticate Look in expensive, powerful colors like black and ivory. She felt rich and wonderful in them. She dyed her hair blond, a very expensive look, but very powerful and intimidating.

At the office no one asked her to lunch anymore, and her husband—the reason for this wonderful change in her lifestyle—didn't really warm up to the way she was dressing.

It was at this point that she consulted me, and I helped her get a better mix in her wardrobe. We bought Gamin looks that were very yummy and expensive, so that she felt good in them. For the office, we added expensively tailored, mix-and-match things in tweed, raw silk, and linen, with wonderful prints included. And I had her change her hair coloring to be highlighted with different colors of blond, a technique that hairdressers call *weaving;* it still looked rich, but it was warmer and more approachable.

Her colleagues at work said, "You must be feeling better!" as if she had been sick. They started asking her to lunch again. And her husband started loving the way she looked.

Do these examples give you a feeling for the potential resource your wardrobe is in supporting your career? These effects are powerful, and they're unconscious.

Let's move on from generalizations now, and talk about how to dress for success in specific careers and other life situations.

Finance

Finance requires the most conservative possible way of dressing—dullness is a positive virtue in the look of people handling other people's money. I advise my men and women clients in jobs like stockbroking, accounting, and investment counseling to invest in just three suits in expensive fabrics and good tailoring; the colors of choice would be navy blue, dark gray, and navy pinstrip. Women could also use a burgundy or dark brick red suit.

I prefer three-piece suits for men; the vest adds power and finish by continuing the color—a Sophisticate Look for men. Men have only two color choices for their shirts, both in oxford cloth: white and blue. Their ties should be dull and conservative—no snowflakes or horse motifs, please. Women can wear pretty little silk bows with their dark suits, and that's the limit of feminine touches. If you have a paperwork day and aren't meeting clients, a herringbone suit is a good choice for the office.

For people in finance, creativity of any sort in their clothes is a bad idea.

Creativity of any sort in your clothes is a bad idea. Your clients want to think of you as utterly stable when you make decisions that affect their personal financial security. You'll have to save the expression of your individuality for your social life and play-clothes.

If you are going to give a speech, you need the credibility of a Sophisticate Look in dark, powerful colors. You've got a whole roomful of clients or colleagues to impress, and the rules apply doubly.

There are two common mistakes that women wearing these strong, conservative looks make: They fail to keep their hair well cut, and they wear too little makeup. If your hair is even a little ragged, you lose the reliable look that you need. Too little makeup against those dark colors will make your face look washed-out and tired, and this not only undermines your credibility, but it is visually out of balance with your strong clothes.

Bankers have somewhat different needs, even though they're in finance. They are on the social side of finance, making contacts for their bank, and it would be accurate to say that they are really in marketing—selling an image and selling financial services. They need to dress very expensively, like everyone in careers related to money, but they can and should selectively wear some Gamin Looks in order to create the friendly, confiding response that anyone in marketing needs. If they're addressing a group, they need the same power looks that any finance person wears; but if they're lunching with a potential high-powered customer, they may want to create informality by wearing a herringbone suit or, for women, a soft patterned blouse.

141

Marketing and Sales

Anyone in marketing or sales should dress for customers—and this requires subtlety. Sometimes you want the customer to relax and confide in you, and sometimes you need to close a sale by being in a strong relationship—the earlier example I gave illustrates this. But you also have to take into consideration what industry or profession the client is in, and make adjustments in your clothing accordingly. I'll give you an example.

Salespeople should adjust their clothes to the industry of their clients.

A corporation in Southern California hired me to work with their sales force because they were having trouble getting to the right people. They were having to make their pitch to secretaries, when they needed to get to corporate buyers—what were they doing wrong? I found out that they were wearing separates in the Southern California casual tradition—sports jackets and slacks. And they were wearing dark raincoats.

I explained to them that the only way they would get to someone powerful in the company was to wear a suit in a dark color. The secretary will automatically feel less powerful than the salesperson and pass him on to someone more powerful. Women can achieve the same effect with a Sophisticate Look. A good color for a saleswoman's first sales call is burgundy, because it has high credibility, but both men and women relate well to it, and you don't know who you're going to be dealing with.

The cheap image of dark raincoats is rather an oddity, since dark colors in most clothes make them appear more expensive. But most people do see them as rather tacky. I think it may be because people who can't afford cleaning bills will get a good dark service-able raincoat, but people with money can afford the cleaning bills for lighter-colored ones. Both men and women should buy only lighter neutrals—beige, camel, or khaki—in their raincoats.

If you are a salesperson who calls on physicians, the problem is different. Doctors work in a more relaxed atmosphere than businesses have, and you have more options. It depends on the price of what you're selling. If you are selling a high-priced computer system, you need to go in with a Sophisticate or Patrician Look in dark colors or burgundy.

But if you are trying to move a service contract from another company to yours, wear a polished Town and Country Look, possibly with a Gamin variation, and they'll talk to you. If the doctor is in a white coat and you walk in wearing a black suit, you're more powerful than he or she is. Choose instead, for example, a navy blazer and gray skirt and white blouse with a soft bow, and the doctor will feel like you're an equal and will tell you about the problems with the current contract holder.

Other professions that respond well to a Town and Country Look in salespeople are academics and technical people like engineers or chemists. Neither group dresses with an emphasis on power, and it's important not to outpower them. People on most campuses or in high-tech companies see three-piece suits only at the highest levels of management, and you may seem like an alien species if you are trying to do business with them wearing an overpowering corporate look.

If you are selling to grade school or high school teachers, you should dress in Gamin Look—children

143

and teenagers always respond well to prints, and so do their teachers. Friendliness and caring about other people is more important than looking overwhelmingly smart here.

The rule for selling is rather like the rule for getting ahead in the office: Dress like your audience but in better quality fabrics. As you move toward closing a sale, however, you may need to increase the power of your look in order to influence the buyer. I would suggest experimenting with this; you may even want to make notes about how your sales calls went with each look you wear. You'll quickly notice trends.

In selling you should dress like your audience but in better quality fabrics.

You also have to dress expensively and powerfully when you are selling high-priced items, adjusting these looks according to your audience. A note about double-breasted suits for men: These are not suitable to business or sales because they give the informal impression of a very rich man at his leisure. There is one exception—the man who sells luxury items like yachts or diamonds; for some reason we like to believe that these people leave Cartier's and have dinner at the yacht club just like their clients. But it would be death for a young executive or a salesman dealing in computers.

Technical and Academic Careers

Academic and technical professionals should dress to look smart rather than businesslike.

Professors, engineers, chemists, and other such highly trained people dress more to look smart than to look powerful or businesslike. The most useful look for those of you in these careers is that of Town and Country separates. Anything that looks too high-fashion or powerful may alienate your colleagues.

144

I once had as a client a chemical engineer who was out of work and having trouble finding a new job. When he came to my office, he had on a neat two-piece suit and nice tie, a useful business look. That was what he was wearing to interviews.

Here's what I told him: Schedule all further interviews for three weeks from now, and in the meantime grow a beard or moustache or both. Get yourself some jeans, and some sports shirts that you'll wear open-necked. Then go interview again.

After he grew his beard and wore his jeans a little bit so they didn't look new, he had three interviews, and he got job offers out of all three. He had looked smart instead of businesslike, and in many job settings, that's what works. If he had been applying for a marketing engineering spot, this would have been a disastrous look, because engineers also have to dress to impress their customers.

If you are a college professor, you'll have to balance this informality with your need to have authority in the classroom. A young woman, in particular, who is not much older than her students, might want to avoid prints and too-casual combinations of separates in lecture situations.

Careers in Creative Fields

If you have a job in fashion, advertising, retail sales, publishing, or the arts, you are in a position to express yourself through your clothes. In fact, in many of these jobs, a conservative look is a handicap—they're asking you to write the world's most original ad copy, and you're wearing a dark blue suit with a little silk bow at the neck? You'll go further if you have a creative look.

Think of the image of some famous creative people, like Georgia O'Keefe, or Andy Warhol, or Paloma Picasso. They have each found a distinctive way of presenting themselves, and this image helps them sell themselves in their careers.

You still need to be selective in how you present your creative image to different audiences. If you are making a presentation to corporate executives, for example, you could wear a conservative suit that they can identify with, but accent it with a tie or jewelry that they wouldn't dream of owning, and wear glasses that are way out on the edge of current eyewear fashion. The beautiful suit assures them that you understand them and their goals, while the other details signal them that you can be trusted to have the fresh new ideas they need.

The Helping Professions

Careers that involve helping people range from many kinds of government careers through social work to receptionist jobs. For all these careers, your best choices are the Gamin and Town and Country looks. That means prints and separates, looks that are low in power and therefore always make people comfortable and more able to tell you what they need.

Gamin and Town and Country Looks are best for people in the helping professions.

A client of mine recently invited me to have lunch with her and several of her colleagues who work in government and Democratic Party positions. The only man of the group was in a diplomatic job, helping people from other countries deal with problems they were having here; he was dressed in a plaid suit with a print tie. The women all had government agency jobs—and all four people were dressed in Gamin Look. They all knew how to project a helpful, friendly image to the people who need them.

Politicians have an interesting dilemma. They need high credibility, so they usually wear dark suits to make speeches; but when they go out into a crowd to meet people and shake hands, they take off their jackets and ties and roll up their sleeves, because they want their constituents to see them as one of themselves who understands them and will help them. They can't switch over suddenly to a Gamin Look just to shake hands, so they make do with informality.

When Geraldine Ferraro was announced as Walter Mondale's choice as running mate on the 1984 Democratic ticket, she had on a red dress with a small print —a Gamin Look that I thought was a surprisingly smart way to present herself as the first U.S. woman ever to be in that high a political position. It made her look friendly, while the color red is a strong, powerful color; I thought it was a look nicely calculated to reassure voters.

Women's Clubs

Women's clubs such as the Junior League and fund-raising efforts like the Cancer Society have a special set of rules—and that's because you're dressing only for other women. The colors you wear, for one thing, can include all the neutrals and subtle tones of olive and oatmeal that women love and men respond so badly to. I have a very expensive olive suit with a suede jacket that I save for Junior League meetings;

When you're dressing only for women you can wear subtle, neutral colors.

147

women sometimes come across a room to compliment me on it. But if I'm around a man in it, there's a good chance he'll say something like, "A pretty woman like you shouldn't wear an ugly outfit like that. . . ."

For society clubs like the Junior League, I would suggest that you wear the Town and Country Look. Women relate very well to this look, and in the expensive versions you should choose, it has the East Coast Old Guard look that works very well here.

Junior League women tend to be very designer-conscious. If you want to be president of the Junior League someday, remember the rule—dress exactly like everyone else, but one level higher in quality. In this case, one level higher means that you always have the expensive, famous-label version of an outfit or jacket rather than the good-quality look-a-likes that would do very well if you have no leadership ambitions. They won't *say* anything, but they'll all know which version you're wearing.

In any of the *big* fundraising groups such as the Cancer Society you need a much more powerful look, so I'd say that you need a Sophisticate or Patrician Look. If you are actually doing fundraising, you are in marketing and should follow the same dress rules that anyone does who's selling something.

The League of Women Voters requires business clothes as if you were in a conservative business career (see the section on Careers in Finance). Evan Picone suits would be good. You need to have a look of power, always keeping in mind that you're dressing for other women. If you want a leadership role, the Sophisticate Look is your only choice.

Corporate Wife—
And Husband!

Men and women who are married to someone in an executive position often have to attend social affairs that are really an extension of their spouse's office life. If you are a corporate wife, you will affect your husband's career by the image you present at these functions. If you are an executive yourself, your husband's image likewise will affect you.

My late husband and I, both with careers of our own, worked out a teamwork approach to these functions that enriched both our careers and our relationship. I would sometimes travel with him to meetings he was running for clients, and the clients' wives would also be present to participate in the meeting's social events. These clients came from small, rural towns, while we came from San Francisco, so I knew that these women would feel prepared to be intimidated by the folks from the Big City. I chose to dress entirely in Gamin Looks with Romantic variations— gingham dresses with little eyelet slips showing, for example.

I got on wonderfully with these women, and since I never mentioned what I did for a living, they imagined me a housewife, but kind of young and nice. They felt more powerful than me, because they at least had on dresses that were all one thing, while my layered looks were unthreatening. They would pass on information to me that was helpful to my husband in working with his clients.

My husband did the same thing when he came to the cocktail parties I held at my office for clients. He would wear patterned Gamin things, and my clients loved talking to him. He would also pick up clues that helped me develop my business effectively.

The way a corporate wife should dress is somewhat dependent on the kind of job her husband has. If you are married to a banker, I would suggest that you wear Nippons, for example. Banking is a social business, and while Nippons are expensive and high-fashion, they're also kind of cute and approachable. If, on the other hand, your husband is the president of a stockbrokerage firm, a better image for you at social functions would be Bill Blass: the expensive classic navy blazer, beautifully cut gabardines, and so on.

If your husband has a high-level position, you need to dress expensively to support his successful image. I recently had a client who was having problems dressing for her husband's career as top executive in a high-tech company. The family had plenty of money —she and her husband and their teenage son all had their own Mercedes. She was dressing in preppy Town and Country Looks that were much too inexpensive and also unflattering to her H-shaped figure. She looked like a secretary who had married her boss, but hadn't learned to dress for her new role.

It became clear to me that the preppy look was deeply ingrained in her self-image, so I put her in Ralph Lauren clothes: They're still preppy, but they have feminine touches and look expensive and high-fashion. They suited her wonderfully, although she had trouble adjusting to their looser look at first. Passersby told her she looked great, and after a few hours looking at similar looks in the stores, she adopted her new look in her own mind. I feel confident that she will now have the right image when she meets her husband's colleagues and their wives.

For social functions related to either your job or your husband's, remember that a Romantic Look can be a very good idea for you. It's a good idea for a woman executive to look feminine on appropriate occasions, just as it's good for a male executive to wear a seersucker suit when he's around employees outside the office. You aren't going to lose your co-workers' respect—they'll just see you as a more human, balanced person with an attractive private life.

A Romantic Look for you at your husband's social events will have a similar effect for him—his co-workers will see him as having balance and a happy home life.

Speaking of a Romantic Look . . .

Dressing for Romance

Most of us have grown up believing that True Love falls out of the sky and fatefully attracts two people who are Meant for Each Other. Mature experience teaches us to doubt the reliability of this belief, because we find out that a whole complex of signals and associations, most of them outside our ability to control them, affect whether a man we like is attracted in turn to us.

151

I have some good news for you: You can influence the progress of a man's attraction to you by the way you dress. Forget all the myths that circulate about sexy clothes; black is not a color that will turn him on in the least, although a black Exotic Look for an important evening out will make him put you on display proudly for other people. But let's start from scratch and review how men feel about clothes.

They don't like those neutral, murky colors that are so attractive to you, and most greens leave them cold, so leave all those colors in the closet if you're going out with someone you like. They like colors that you can easily put a name to, and pink, peach, and red are especially attractive to them. If you want men to talk to you at parties or when you travel, pick something in one of these three colors.

They love soft textures, especially angora. If you need cheering up and want your husband to cherish you tonight, put on a peachy angora sweater and see what happens.

For some reason, men seem to think certain patterns are sexy, patterns that women could study all day and never see what the attraction is. I have a brightly striped blouse that I wore to lunch with a date; he called me up in the afternoon to make sure I didn't change before he took me out to dinner, because he loves that blouse. And this is a blouse that I don't even like very much.

Men are pleased to be with a woman other people like, and that means wearing Gamin in social situations.

Another thing to remember is that men are very pleased to be with a woman that other people like, and that of course means that wearing a Gamin Look when you're with him in social situations is a very good idea. Let me tell you the story of a wedding I've just been invited to.

I have a client in Maine whose family is very, very rich. She's a divorcee, and when she came to me for help, she said she'd found a man she wanted to marry, but that there were some problems to overcome. He is a high school coach with no independent means, and her wealth naturally keeps him from thinking of her very seriously. He was not even showing any signs of being very interested in her.

Like many wealthy women, she wore almost exclusively the Town and Country Look, which women relate wonderfully to, but men find unappealing in most of its variations. She had no Gamin or Romantic looks in her wardrobe.

The plan I gave her was this: To catch his attention she should wear Gamin Looks. Once that's accomplished, she should court him with Romantic clothes. Then to get him to the point of actually proposing, she should use a little bit of Sophisticate Look for a businesslike response.

We went shopping and bought her a lot of soft prints in a Laura Ashley tradition, layered, with lacy blouses. She looked absolutely wonderful. One of the Romantic outfits was a very lacy off-white linen dress with a pink sash to be worn low on the hips— wonderful. She had discovered that pink was his favorite color, so we unabashedly added a lot of pink to her closet. For the Sophisticate Look, we bought her a beautiful pink suit.

The first thing he took her to was a track meet, and she wore one of her pretty Gamin outfits in a soft print. All the kids talked to her and loved her, and so did their parents when they came around to pick up their children. This was a new experience for her, because in her expensive Town and Country clothes she had looked like she owned the town (which she does); in her new clothes, she looked like a nice, friendly woman and for the most part they didn't realize who she was. She was asked to help out by driving kids home, and she had a great time. Her coach started to fall in love with her because his kids thought she was great.

Next he invited her out to a dinner party, and she wore a pink gingham dress, which is laying Gamin on extra thick. She looked at herself in the mirror and thought it was disgustingly sweet, but she recovered from her reservations when she saw how much he wanted to be near her—he would hardly leave her side all night. All the Town and Country women came over to talk to her, and she felt vibrant and alive—it was such a nice change from having people be intimidated by her. That night he kissed her for the first time, and she realized that it was time to bring on the Romantic Looks.

When they went to a shower for friends of his that were getting married, she pulled out the off-white linen dress with its pink sash and pretty little matching pink shoes. When he saw what she was wearing they barely made it on to the party. At this point in their relationship he started asking her what kind of jewelry she liked and discussing permanence.

It was time for the pink suit, a Sophisticate Look for seriously discussing business. This is an expensive suit with a raw silk jacket, pants, and matching blouse, all in the same gorgeous pink fabric.

She invited him to dinner, saying that there were some things she wanted to talk over with him, but she didn't know how she was going to introduce the topic she had in mind. It was no problem—as soon as he walked in the door he automatically became businesslike and asked for pencil and paper. He started making a list about his life goals, his plans for selling his house, and what he wanted to do for the next several years. He did everything but propose.

I suggested that she wear a black suit with a Romantic Look to the next social occasion with him. She sensed that he was still observing how she related to other people. The black color made her look serious, and the Romantic Look countered that with femininity. It was a group in which she knew all the women, and since women relate well to black, she continued to be a social success. Afterward he said, "I'm so proud to be with you. Everybody likes you—kids love you, adults like you."

They're now engaged. She had a pink wedding dress chosen—after all, it's a second marriage. But he wants her to wear white, because he sees her as having a lot of innocence.

Dressing for Homemaking

Probably the women who have the hardest time figuring out what to wear are those who are home with children. Their lives are divided between time spent with children and time spent with adults, and a casual look is almost always the most appropriate.

I find that housewives often fall into the trap of owning only clothes at the two extremes—t-shirts with jeans for everything they do during the day, and clothes that are too dressy for most of their going-out occasions and end up gathering dust in the closet.

If this describes you, I would suggest that you plan a wardrobe based on variations of the Town and Country Look. When you're with children, you need practical fabrics—they'll make a mess of suede and leather, no matter how fashionable these materials are at the moment. Find cotton and easy-care fabrics and put them together in a fun way. Children will love you in bright colors and prints.

When you're with adults, you can mix your practical separates with a few well-chosen other pieces, depending on who you're going to be with. For example, if you are going to be around male friends of your husband, you might wear a red plaid shirt with gray slacks for a Gamin variation that would make them feel very comfortable. Or if you were going to be with women friends, you could wear combinations of solid separates in more elegant fabrics, perhaps a red silk dress with a white silk knit sweater vest. Because both pieces are solids and both colors are impressive, you would make your presence felt.

If you choose your separates correctly, you should be able to find several ways to combine them for evenings out.

Because you are not in a structured business situation, it's not necessary for you to wear suits—dresses and skirts are more appropriate for your social life. If you choose your separates correctly, you should be able to find several ways to combine them for evenings out, and if you don't always see the same people, one smashing Exotic Look would take you everywhere really dressy.

Don't forget the importance of dressing for your husband. If he sees you in a terrycloth robe when he leaves every morning, and then finds you in jeans and a t-shirt every evening when he gets home, your

156

love life might not be worth living! Try an angora sweater or silk shirt over those jeans—believe me, when a woman changes to something soft just for her man, it's a real turn-on.

Pregnancy deserves clothes that will give you a lift. Don't get stuck in the rut of over-blouses with jeans, or by the time the baby comes you and your husband may both want to run away from home. Laura Ashley clothes, which are mostly Gamin and Romantic Look, cheer pregnant mothers up wonderfully—not to mention the prospective fathers. Have fun with colors and prints and wonderful fabrics so that you still feel pretty and lovable while your waistline expands.

Try It Out for Yourself

Are you having trouble believing that clothes are as powerful as I've suggested? Certainly life is very complex, and clothes cannot exclusively achieve any result you have in mind. But *do not underestimate the amazing unconscious effect that clothes have on people.* Try these theories out for yourself and observe the results you get. I predict that you'll realize that, without your knowing it, your clothes have been affecting what happens to you every day.

Without your knowing it, your clothes have been affecting what happens to you every day.

Now you have the information you need to make your clothes work for you: You can create credibility when you have something important to say, reduce conflict when you need to, have a friendly happy day, and encourage the man in your life to see the wonderful, loving qualities you knew you had all along.

You're ready to go shopping!

7. Go Shopping

If you identified with the shopping panic of the woman in Chapter 1, you're ready now to break with your past errors, and make a plan for a wardrobe that will really present you to the world with the image you choose.

You've defined your figure's characteristics and how to dress accordingly; you've outlined your life-style and considered what demands it makes on your wardrobe; you know about the Seven Looks that are available for you to work with; and you know which of the three fashion cycles you should currently be shopping for. You're ready to do your wardrobe inventory.

Open your closet and all your drawers and carefully consider each item. What do you already have in your wardrobe that you will want to continue to wear? What can you add to those pieces to give yourself more variety? What about that good-looking navy skirt with nothing to match it but a few separate blouses? Perhaps you can add other pieces in the same navy dye lot to create a finished look that will mix nicely with other things you have or will buy.

Open your closet and all your drawers and carefully consider each item.

Remember to review *all* of your wardrobe needs. Do you have enough clothes for the office but nothing to wear for evenings out, or for casual weekend outings? Or do you have plenty of playclothes but not much that makes you feel like the public woman you are or would like to become?

Setting Your Budget

When you have finished inventorying everything you can continue to use and everything you need to add, you must decide on your wardrobe budget. I suggest to my clients that they go over all of their checks and bills for the past year and see how much they spent on their wardrobe over that period of time. Better still, you may even want to go back three years—and what you find out will probably astonish you! You may have either bought too much at too high a price for the pleasure you got, or you may not have bought enough, and your wardrobe is suffering from starvation. Either extreme is dangerous over a long period of time, tempting you into panic buying and expensive mistakes to relieve the stress you feel from not having the right clothes when you need them.

Remember the effect of the five-year cycles when you consider how much you should spend this year. My clients spend the bulk of their wardrobe money the first and second year of a new cycle. In the third year they add a few pieces of jewelry, perhaps replace some blouses, add to their evening wardrobe, or buy casual playclothes. In the fourth and fifth years they buy little or nothing while looking for the clues that are starting to appear to indicate the direction of the next cycle.

If you find yourself with few clothes and you are in the middle of a cycle, you may want to make fewer and more disciplined purchases, saving some money to buy a wider wardrobe later when clothing lines in the new cycle start appearing. If you have a really good eye, you may be able to buy some transition pieces that will work in both the present and future cycles.

Where to Shop

The best areas for shopping are in large cities. Suburban stores and shopping centers, no matter how beautiful and expensive their lines, are not as effective. Why? Because in cities the buyers must cater to shoppers from all over the world—shoppers with a wide range of tastes, figure types, budgets, and lifestyles. In suburban areas stores cater to the average customer in their locale; they also have fewer total customers and must limit their stock accordingly.

For example, in a given manufacturer's line on the rack in a suburban store, you might find a nice pair of black slacks, a print blouse, and a solid jacket—but not necessarily all in your size. In the city you will also find that line's skirt, often with a choice of more than one style in any given color, as well as a solid sweater and several choices of blouses to match or blend with the outfit.

Convinced? Even if the large city nearest you is a day away, it's worth the extra effort—we're talking about an important personal investment. Even the cost of a hotel room is modest in comparison with the cost of mistakes and compromises that limit the value of your investment.

Even if the large city nearest you is a day away, it's worth the extra effort.

The Sophisticate Method of Wardrobe Strategy

I have mentioned my theory of clothes buying in several places earlier in this book, but let's review it now that you're getting down to business. I call my approach the Sophisticate Method, because it starts with buying a complete Sophisticate Look. Your first purchase should be every piece you can possibly find in a solid color of the exact same dye lot. You can do this by staying within a given label, but if you have a good eye and look at the colors in natural light, you can match successfully between manufacturers.

Your first purchase should be every piece you can possibly find in a solid color of the exact same dye lot.

You should expect to go to as many as four or five stores to do this. Typically, each store buys several pieces in a given line, but not the whole line; another store will buy a slightly different group; and a third store yet another selection—all from the same designer or manufacturer. If you're savvy enough to shop carefully in all these stores, you'll be able to get a complete selection that will add tremendously to the effectiveness of your wardrobe in future years.

Your second step is to identify a line of print pieces that will mix well with the solid color you just invested in.

Your second step is to identify a line of print pieces that will mix well with the solid color you just invested in. For example, if you started with navy blue in every possible piece, you already have several versions of the Sophisticate Look available to you. If you now add all the pieces you can find in a navy, green, and cream plaid, you have several Town and Country Looks: the plaid blouse with the navy skirt or pants and jacket; the plaid skirt with the navy blouse and plaid jacket; or even the plaid pants with the navy blouse and navy jacket.

Is one of the blouses you already own a good-looking navy and cream pin-dot blouse? Put this together with your plaid suit for a Gamin variation, or give yourself another Town and Country Look by wearing it with the navy pieces. Or mix the pin-dot blouse with the plaid skirt and navy jacket. See what variety is now available to you?

The next step is another Sophisticate Look, this time in a solid color that goes with both the print and original solid color. How about a camel two-piece dress, jacket, shoes, and belt? Now you can make a Patrician Look for yourself; wear your camel dress, navy belt, navy jacket, and camel shoes—two of each color. Or wear the camel jacket with the plaid skirt and navy blouse. . . . See?

The next step is another Sophisticate Look, this time in a solid color that goes with both the print and original solid color.

When your money is limited, you may be tempted not to follow my plan of buying every piece in the same color, then everything available in a coordinating pattern; don't imagine that buying a little of this and a little of that is going to give a limited wardrobe *more* variety—the opposite is in fact true. You will have more limited combinations and a more limited number of looks for the varying events you need to dress for. Variety can be achieved more effectively through your accessories—jewelry, scarves, belts, handbags, shoes, and even stockings.

Don't ever buy just one of something. I am so strict about this in my own wardrobe that I won't even buy a blouse without buying all of the matching pieces in its color tones. Experience tells me that I cannot justify the expense of a single blouse because it will leave gaps in my wardrobe. As a result, everything in my closet works with everything else, and when I travel,

Don't ever buy just one of something.

Everything in
my closet works
with everything
else, and it's easy
to pack.

it's easy to pack and I only need one or two suitcases to allow for all the variations I'll need to dress appropriately for every situation.

Remember the Four Shopping Sins in Chapter 1? Single-item purchasing was one of them. I've started thinking of this approach as the Town and Country Method of Wardrobe Strategy—it's the one that stores encourage you to use, because it keeps you coming back again and again to buy yet another separate piece. This method is a truly disorganized manner of purchasing clothing, and you'll never be quite satisfied with the result.

Using Accessories to Create Variety

Accesories are essential to complete each color group in your wardrobe—but they can also be used to blend color tones together in unusual combinations. I have a bright red skirt in my wardrobe with all the matching pieces. I also have a complete set in turquoise. But I'd never been able to put the two together in an eye-pleasing way. Then I ran across a good-looking shawl with a turquoise background and red design in the center. Now when I wear my red blouse, red skirt, and turquoise-and-red shawl, I get many compliments. But I can also wear my turquoise blouse with my red pants and red coat, tossing the shawl over the coat to create a very unusual but dressier look.

You can't count on finding the correct accessory for two unusual colors in your wardrobe—you could look your whole life and never carry out what seemed like a good idea. But I like to add to my wardrobe by *starting* with a great accessory—a scarf, belt, necklace, shoes, or purse that blends two unusual colors together; then I purchase both colors in totality to mix around many different ways. You'll be amazed at how creative you can be when you have a roadmap to follow.

I like to add to my wardrobe by starting with a great accessory.

When I travel, I often concentrate on buying accessories. They're easy to bring back in a suitcase, you can find unusual things by local artisans, and you may be able to buy the very things that are hardest to find at home.

You can run into trouble if you buy pieces in a color without filling out the entire color group; dye lots differ tremendously from city to city and year to year —if you don't finish your color group within six months, you may be out of luck for several years.

Line Variation

We've talked a lot about having variation in color and look in your wardrobe. You should also make sure that you don't have more than one jacket, blazer, skirt, or dress in the same style. It's just as important to have line differentiation in your wardrobe as it is to have differences in color. If everything you wear looks the same, you'll get bored, and the people you see every day will literally stop looking at you.

It's as important to have line differentiation in your wardrobe as it is to have differences in color.

It's easy to fall into the pattern of buying the same line over and over again; you succeeded with it once, and believe that it's the best or only line that works well with your figure. This is never true—everyone, regardless of figure type, can wear a variety of current styles; it's only true that not everyone can wear exactly the same variations of each style.

If you find yourself falling into the habit of buying the same safe uniform over and over, review Chapter 2 and identify your body type. Remind yourself of what lines are good on you, and then take the time to find the style variation that works for your figure. This is another good reason to shop in the city instead of the smaller shopping areas—you *need* the variety of lines available in stores catering to a broader clientele.

Smart Shopping

Give yourself plenty of time for serious shopping; an investment that you expect to last for the next three to five years needs careful consideration. Avoid shopping when you have the pressure of a trip or important appointment that you're hurrying to buy clothes for; you'll make compromises when you buy under pressure, and regret it when you find something better a month later.

I suggest to my clients that they take several possible purchases home, then decide under their own lights, and wearing the correct makeup, underwear, and accessories, what pieces will work best over the longest period of time. It's much easier to concentrate in the privacy of your own home than in a small, badly lighted dressing room, especially if you're being pressured by an impatient sales clerk.

Shop alone or with a professional consultant. You need to take your time and work in an uninterrupted atmosphere. You can't let your concentration be disturbed by a friend's pacing around, wondering why you're taking so long and when you'll be willing to stop for lunch.

Investment dressing should be fun, and *can* be if it's done properly. But if shopping is the most confusing and painful thing you do each year, it would be better for you to hire a private wardrobe consultant to do your shopping for or with you.

When I take on a client, I follow these steps: I do a lifestyle workup on her; I go through her closet to see what she has; and I help her budget her wardrobe needs over a five-year period. Because I am in the stores nearly every day somewhere in the country, I know where things are, what the newest and best lines are, and how to fit the client's lifestyle with what is available in her size and figure needs. In many cases I can plan an entire season's wardrobe in a matter of two to four hours. Until you have a lot of practice, it may take you weeks to plan and carry out your strategy, and you take the chance of making many mistakes and missing many opportunities.

Now that you've finished this book, you have at your command all the principles of sound wardrobe strategy—and you now know that being well-dressed is a lot more complex and subtle than just putting clothes on your body. You also know how to plan for the psychological messages you're giving, how to manage people's impressions of you, how fashion cycles affect your clothing choices, and how to coordinate and expand your wardrobe purchases.

You're ready to let Suzie Woodward's Wardrobe Strategy work for *you!*

If shopping is the most confusing and painful thing you do, hire a private wardrobe consultant.

Index

Now that you've read the book . . . .
Stay on top of wardrobe fashions
with this NEWSLETTER

Suzie's bimonthly **Wardrobe Strategy NEWSLETTER**will give you immediate up-dates on what's happening in the fashion world throughout the year—and put it all in perspective with what you've learned from reading the book.

Each issue contains a feature article on what to look for now, one or two pieces on related topics (such as make-up and hair, accessories, seasonal color changes, and correct timing), Suzie's reader question-and-answer section, and ''your astrological forecast.''

Volume 1 begins with the September/October 1984 issue and ends with the July/August 1985 issue. Your subscription will begin with the issue of the month your order is received (back issues are available on request).

- -